The Goose

COPYRIGHT © 1996 BIBLIOTHECA CULINARIA S.R.L., LODI

GRAPHIC AND EDITORIAL COORDINATION: MARIO CUCCI
COMPILATION AND TEXTS: DANIELA GARAVINI
GRAPHICS AND DESIGN: THE C' SERVIZI EDITORIALI SAS, MILAN
PHOTOGRAPHS: NICOLETTA INNOCENTI
OTHER ILLUSTRATIONS: "ACHILLE BERTARELLI" PRINT COLLECTION, NATURAL HISTORY LIBRARY, MILAN

COPYRIGHT © 1998 FOR THE ENGLISH-LANGUAGE EDITION
KÖNEMANN VERLAGSGESELLSCHAFT MBH
BONNER STR. 126, D-50968 KÖLN

ENGLISH TRANSLATION: KATE CLAYTON/ROS SCHWARTZ TRANSLATIONS, LONDON
EDITING/TYPESETTING: GRAPEVINE PUBLISHING SERVICES, LONDON
PRODUCTION MANAGER: DETLEV SCHAPER
ASSISTANT: NICOLA LEURS
PRINTING AND BINDING: KOSSUTH PRINTING HOUSE CO.
PRINTED IN HUNGARY
ISBN 3-8290-1464-3
10 9 8 7 6 5 4 3 2 1

HISTORY, FOLKLORE, ANCIENT RECIPES

The Goose

34 recipes by Germano Pontoni
41 recipes by Italy's most famous chefs

Foreword by Licio Damiani
Preface by Corrado Barberis
Introduction by Rossano Nistri
Wines recommended by Claudio Carboni

An animal that captures the flavor of the past

LICIO DAMIANI

All along the ditches and across the threshing-yards the air was full of the beating of white wings while my ears were filled with the sound of that raucous squawking, those rasping screeches. Childhood memories of trips to the countryside are inextricably bound up with the image of those great web-footed birds waddling along, clownishly belligerent, ungainly cousins of the regal swans.

During World War II the goose was a walking larder. My grandmother used to raise two or three. It was agonizing to watch her stuff them with maize, forcing it through a funnel down the long neck held fast between the legs of their torturer. But I never had the courage to watch them being slaughtered; one day the animal would appear, dangling lifeless but still fascinating in its soft, thick cloud of plumage. And then there would be the dead body plucked bare of its feathers, plump and enormous, waiting to be gutted.

The golden-yellow goose fat extracted from the guts like gold from a mine was manna for the whole family. The terrine it was stored in became a treasure-chest. Unlike today, there were no cares about diets, cholesterol and triglycerides. Goose fat sizzled in abundance in our pots and pans, and when we had colds or flu we would smear some on our chests.

The goose is an animal that embodies the flavor of the past in every sense. Every schoolchild learns about the famous incident of the Capitoline geese, sacred to Juno, that saved Rome by raising the alarm as the Gauls approached. And school history books would always have a picture showing the barbarian warrior cowering in fear before the screeching geese defying him with wide open beaks. In the eyes of an elementary school pupil the birds seemed to shed their humble, bucolic status, becoming imbued with epic heroism.

Pliny the Elder celebrated the goose for its keen sense of hearing: "Even when the dogs sleep, the goose watches." Other Roman authors, however, preferred to dwell more on the animal's nutritious qualities: "Rusticus gratus est" (the goose is particularly dear to the farmers), wrote Lucio Giunio Moderato Columella in his treatise *De Agricoltura*. Those who offered advice on the raising and feeding of geese, on their habitat, and on fattening methods include Cato, Varro, Celso and Palladio. *"The goose cannot easily be reared without water nor without much grass; it is harmful in places that have been sown with seed or planted with trees because it plucks off all the tender shoots it can reach. But wheresoever there is a stream or a lake and abundance of grass, and the fields that have been sown are quite far away, there can this bird also be reared."*

One of the best areas for rearing geese was the countryside around Aquileia. The historian Strabo refers to the goose-herds and goose-fatteners of Aquileia, the *anserarii*, mentioning that their skills were in demand as far away as Rome and that they made their way there herding immense flocks. A great stream of birds crossed woods and countryside to reach the city. For the Romans, the most highly prized part of the goose was its large liver, or *ficatum*, and to ensure that it reached the desired weight the animal was fattened with figs.

Apicius, the gourmet and gluttonous author of *De re coquinaria*, an invaluable book of recipes, advises that the liver should be cut into slices, marinated in garum (fish sauce) together with pepper, lovage, and two bay leaves, wrapped in a net, and roasted on a grill; but he instructs not to neglect the meat, which should be served boiled, also with a mixture of pepper, lovage, coriander seed, mint, rue, the indispensable garum, and extra virgin oil.

In the famous feast that occupies such a large part of Petronius' *Satyricon*, the goose makes its appearance adorning the sign of Aquarius in a spectacular course of the meal representing all the constellations of the Zodiac.

The bird continued to enjoy (if that is the word) great success in the rural economy of the Middle Ages. It appears in all the treatises, listed among the spit roasts. Its velvety, smooth flesh was flavored with aromatic herbs soaked in oil and accompanied with sauces, orange juice or lemon. The custom of serving goose on All Saints' Day in Italy, and for the feast of St Martin in northern Europe, has survived to this day.

The cooks of the Paris neighborhoods of Saint Merri and Saint Séverin were famous for the skill with which they prepared goose. They would fatten the bird before roasting, carve it to perfection, and use the offal to whip up a cold dish to savor while waiting for the goose to cook. Parisians gave *pâté de foie gras* its fame and made it a triumph of French gastronomy. But the goose has more to offer. The soft voluptuousness of its down used for filling duvets and quilted jackets enfolds the user in the lightest of warm, sensual embraces. Its quills make pens of immaculate elegance, used by writers and clerks, and they are also an aristocratic, romantic and literary symbol. Interwoven goose feathers once made fire-fans to fan the flames in the fireplaces of the nobility, and white feathers rise proudly above the heads of the officers of the Swiss Guard.

The goose, in short, is a fairytale blend of history, economy and memories as cosy as goose down itself. But the goose also stands for stupidity; for some reason, folk tradition has made the goose a symbol of crassness.

The Goose

CORRADO BARBERIS

President of the National Institute of Rural Sociology

In October 1987, I wrote in the preface of Germano Pontoni's book *Il libro dell'oca* (*The Book of the Goose*):

"A string of lucky events introduced me to the group of 'apostles' in Viscone di Chiopris so ardently devoted to reviving the goose in Friuli. Antonello Pesot is the St Peter of this little 'church', but its St Paul is Germano Pontoni: he is truly the 'ideologue' capable of transforming a taste into an intellectual adventure and of establishing the cultural weight and substance of a dish by the quality of browned or roasted skin.

"He gave ample proof of his talents as a cook during the memorable 'Goose Dinner' organized in Rome on December 8, 1986 at Patrizia and Roberto's restaurant, Pianeta Terra, close by the National Institute of Rural Sociology, and he will undoubtedly demonstrate his skills again on many occasions, proclaiming the excellence of the recipes created by his peerless consort Mamma Bertilla. Poet, philosopher and the goose's own

historian, Pontoni now brings us a piece of writing that positively oozes with flavor like droplets of fat trickling into a dripping pan, until every line is crisp but every page is left meltingly soft. Fascinated by the Italy of memory and reminiscence, he now faithfully restores to us all the fragrance of an ancient, lost Friuli."

It may well be that in order to bring out all the qualities of the goose and goose products, raising awareness and appreciation of the bird, what is needed is an exercise in gastronomic archaeology and an economic

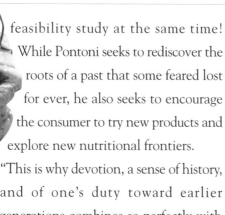

feasibility study at the same time! While Pontoni seeks to rediscover the roots of a past that some feared lost for ever, he also seeks to encourage the consumer to try new products and explore new nutritional frontiers.

"This is why devotion, a sense of history, and of one's duty toward earlier generations combines so perfectly with commercial success, demonstrating that culture is a form of erudition highly skilled in the art of transforming itself into money – a fact that far from being blameworthy is positively desirable. The 'apostles of Friuli' are not alone in this undertaking but combine their efforts with another 'patriarchate' based at Mortara; while at the same time – also thanks to their timely missionary zeal – other initiatives are springing up in other regions of Italy.

"So it seems that the time is ripe to draw up an inventory of our available gastronomic heritage. And this 'state of the art' account of the noble goose has been created thanks to Germano Pontoni."

Since then, the goose has come a long way in Italian gastronomy. In his *Natural History*, Pliny describes how entire flocks were herded from the land of the Morini – today's Pas de Calais on the shores of the English Channel – toward Rome; nowadays the journey that geese make is less ambitious and generally concerns only products that have already been processed or canned. It has taken until the 1990s for those hosting receptions in Rome to serve breast of goose, cured goose "hams" and goose salami without such dishes causing any raised eyebrows except by their excellence. And thanks to the initiative of Gioacchino Palestro a pure goose "ecumenical salami" has now been created, with a bill placed before parliament by Giacomo de Ghislanzoni Cardoli to award it a D.O.C.

An ideal habitat for geese has a lake or river and grass alongside.

(*denominazione d'origine controllata* – controlled region of origin status) alongside the traditional Mortara version containing a cooked goose-and-pork mixture. This salami follows an ancient Jewish recipe not unlike one that used to be known in Friuli as "Grandma Sara's"; the real novelty lies in the fact that for the first time an object of gluttony has been accorded recognition as an instrument of culture and peace, since it can be happily eaten, without scruple, by Christians, Jews, and Muslims, followers of the three great monotheistic religions. Precisely because it is a symbol of peace, this salami is the first to have received honorary Italian citizenship through the good offices of the professor who gave it its name: the event took place in Mortara on September 29, 1996. Since then, whoever eats goose – aided and abetted, I hope, by the recipes brought together here by Pontoni and some forty other established chefs – can truly be said to be eating culture!

A long history of goose and mankind

Rossano Nistri

In his *Natural History*, Pliny, like every other erudite Latin writer, refers to the goose using the term *anser*. In everyday speech, however, the rural Italians of the later Roman Empire called the bird *auca*, using a word said to be derived from *avica*, possibly the diminutive of *avis* (bird). As is often the case, it was the popular term that remained in common use in the Italian language while the Classical term gives us the scientific name for this particular soft-feathered, web-footed animal.

All the domestic varieties of goose are descended from *Anser anser*, commonly known as the graylag goose, from which they have been bred since several thousand years BC.

> **NAMES**
>
> Scientific name of the main genus: *Anser*.
>
> Other genera: *Branta, Caloephaga, Cereopsis, Plectropterus.*
> Italian: oca
> French: oie
> English: goose
> Spanish: ganso, oca
> Portuguese: ganso
> Hungarian: sud
> German: Gans
> Russian: rycb
> Dutch: gans

Like the pig, the goose was judged by the ancients, and indeed up to the mid-20th century, to be a highly profitable animal. Every part of it was used. As well as the meat and the liver, its feathers were prized as was its fat. Parts such as the giblets were used for stews of various kinds, and the neck used either to make sausages for immediate consumption (the stuffed neck of our grandmothers' recipes) or salamis that would keep for long periods of time. The feet, which according to Pliny were considered a delicacy by his contemporary Messalino Cotta, are still highly sought-after today in certain areas of southern France.

For thousands of years, this ungainly waddler, the web-footed Mother Goose, an archetypal figure in the collective imagination, has been the incarnation of abundance, providing protein and energy and, through its plumage, warmth and love. It has become part of the marriage rituals of the peoples of northern Europe and been incorporated into rites of purification as a propitiative element; it plays a role in hundreds of feast days, festivals and popular games, such as the *Contrada dell'Oca*, or Goose Quarter, of Siena (with its strong totemic connotations) and the Palio of Mortara as well as all those other rowdy festivals in which competitors strive to outdo one another in daring jumps and acrobatic feats so as to yank the bird's head off its neck (nowadays the geese are mercifully butchered beforehand). It is also the ancestor of every board game; the *gioco dell'oca* or *jeu de l'oie* (similar to snakes and ladders) is a direct link between our own childhoods and that of Louis XII of France. All these things are still with us, reminding us in their symbolism of society's periodic, expiatory need to kill a king or queen. When

the king is dead, even if only in the frying pan or on the spit, long live the king!

THE WILD GOOSE

The enormous black V-shapes that can be seen crossing our skies in late fall and in spring are made by flocks of wild geese flying in formation at the time of their seasonal migration. Though life is by no means easy for them, a few dozen different species of wild geese still survive on our planet. Every year, with the exception of those species such as the spur-winged goose, the Nile goose, the Hawaiian ne-ne and the lesser white-fronted goose, whose natural habitat is in subtropical countries, geese leave their territories in northern Europe, North America, Siberia and the Arctic cliffs where they nest and fly south in vast groups, covering thousands of miles to spend the winter in more temperate climes. The seasonal migration of these noisy flocks is the stuff of dreams for hunters who flout the ban imposed by law in almost every country and lie in wait to give the geese a bloody welcome.

Generally, the birds belonging to the genus *Anser* are larger than those of the other genera that make up the *Anatidae* (the goose family). The males of all the species are larger than the females. Although they can be identified by characteristics common to all *Anatidae*, individuals of the various species differ in size, from the 21 in (55 cm) of the red-breasted goose to the 32-35 in (80-90 cm) of the graylag goose; in weight, from the 2½ lb (1.2 kg) of the barnacle goose to the 13 lb (6 kg) of the Danube goose; and in the length of their legs, which in the spur-winged goose can measure up to 32-35 in (80-90 cm).

The color of the plumage can vary, according to the species, from the pure white of the snow goose through infinite shades of gray and brown to the gray-black-brown of the Hawaiian ne-ne. Many varieties sport a wide range of colored markings and rings.

The adult of what might be called the generic goose – the *Anser anser* of Linnaeus' classification, which is also known as the *Anser ferus*, *Anser cinerus* or *Oca Paglietana* – has an average length of some 33 in (85 cm) and weighs 5-8½ lb (2.5-4 kg).

Its coloring is gray-brown with white streaks and with blackish-brown feathers at the tips of the wings. The beak is orange, the legs and feet a bright flesh-color and the claws are black.

NATURAL HISTORY

A member of the family *Anatidae*, the goose has much in common with the duck and the swan but is nevertheless distinguished from them by a number of important characteristics, primarily the shape of the head, which is smaller and more compact than those of the other web-footed species, and the beak, which is the same length as the rest of the head.

Unlike the duck, the beak of the goose is deeper than it is wide at the base. It has a cutting edge, ideal for shearing through the leaves, grass, shoots and small plants on which it feeds. The upper jaw is also equipped with subconical cartilagenous lamellae along the lateral edges; toward the outside these become denticles enabling the goose to carry out a sort of basic chewing of the plants that it eats. In the swan and the duck, on the other hand, these same lamellae retain their original function (typical in the structure of the mouthparts of aquatic birds) and act as a filter serving to strain out particles of food and plankton.

The goose's rather short limbs and portly body give it a somewhat awkward, waddling gait typical of a bird who, unlike the duck, has abandoned its natural habitat in the water, but whose body on the other hand has not yet evolved to suit it to an exclusively terrestrial life. It is precisely for this reason that, although it is a very able swimmer, the goose is essentially herbivorous and therefore prefers to live in marshy areas and bogs; the webbing of its feet is less extensive than that of the duck or swan because it has less need than its aquatic cousins to be able to perform a rowing action. Its broad, curved wings with their extended tertiary flight feathers are designed not for rapid flight but for the sustained flight at high altitudes (geese are capable of overflying the Himalayas) required for the journeys that they make – sometimes covering vast distances – during their annual migration.

ETHOLOGY

Popular wisdom attributes a number of negative qualities to these great lumbering, web-footed birds with their easy-going air and voracious appetites. A variety of expressions familiar in  every part of Europe and America, such as "to be a silly goose", "have the brain of a goose" or "cackling like a gaggle of geese", assume the goose to be obtuse, vacuous and irritatingly noisy.

At the same time, however, the goose is surrounded by a number of ancient stories that border on myth and legend. Although they are drawn from the selfsame well of popular wisdom that has given rise to the prejudice of the goose's stupidity, they pay tribute to the squawking and flapping anserine guards that supposedly saved the Capitol and the City of Rome itself from a nocturnal attack by the Celtic hordes of Brenno in 380 BC, implying (beneath the irony that can be read into a victory over the Gauls achieved thanks to a flock of geese) that the birds had an intelligent attachment to their owners.

Modern ethology, beginning with the acute observations of Konrad Lorenz, describes an animal by no means obtuse, although it is indeed voracious and lazy (the goose spends around half its day resting while it digests its food). It is easily domesticated, having a sort of social relation with people almost like that of a child to its parents; this has developed over the course of thousands of years, growing from what ethologists refer to as a "primary stimulus" – that is, the drive that causes the goose to follow and regard as its protector whatever figure it first sees after hatching.

This is not, then, a particularly foolish bird but nor is it more intelligent than others. It is simply a creature whose own instinctive behavior and innate responses have become structured into its own unique code of relations and communication during the course of its evolution, just like any other animal. The explanations offered by Lorenz himself in relation to the different calls and other sounds uttered by the goose are exemplary in this regard: these can be interpreted, as

it were, in terms of asking questions, giving information, calling for help and a number of highly specific appeals and exhortations that are understood by all individuals of the same species and that are capable of functioning as a proper language, albeit an extremely simplified one.

THE GOOSE AS LIVESTOCK

With the exception of the common goose, which rarely exceeds 8½ lb (4 kg) in weight, geese belonging to the species selected over the course of thousands of years for rearing as domestic and industrial livestock are a great deal larger and heavier than their wild counterparts. An adult male Emden goose, fully fattened, can even reach a weight of 33 lb (15 kg). Their plumage is a bright, pure white throughout, with the exception of the gray Padua goose, a few examples of the common goose and the female of the Normandy goose, whose plumage contains various shades of gray and whose down is therefore not considered worth collecting. The commercially viable strains are generally divided into three categories according to the main productive use to which they are put: meat and liver; lean meat; skins and feathers.

Among the geese raised for purposes of meat and *foie gras*

Although it is an aquatic bird, the goose feeds mainly on grass, leaves and various plants.

production (the Toulouse goose is a perfect example), the farm birds raised in large open spaces with ample opportunity for movement have an agile, muscular build. They provide excellent meat and reach a weight of 17-22 lb (8-10 kg) for the male and 13-17 lb (6-8 kg) for the female. Factory-farmed birds intended for the production of *foie gras*, which are force fed and kept in confined spaces, have thickset, fat bodies that tend to become deformed with age. Their flesh is very fatty and they can reach a weight of 26-30 lb (12-14 kg) for the male and 20½ -26 lb (9-12 kg) for the female. The liver can weigh over 21 oz (600 g).

Geese reared for lean meat fare best in the open and so are of average size, weighing 11-19½ lb (5-9 kg). Apart from producing meat of excellent quality, these birds are used to improve the hardiness and resistance of the other liver-producing strains by means of judicious cross-breeding.

Geese raised for their plumage provide an average of 14-17 oz (400-500 g) of down a head, which is collected at intervals through the year. The breeds selected for this purpose, like those used to supply swan's-down for the fur trade for such items as trimming and powder puffs, are not fattened, so as prevent fatty infiltrations in the cutaneous tissues.

EARLY EVIDENCE OF DOMESTICATION

There is evidence that geese were domesticated as early as 5000 years BC, undoubtedly earlier than hens and other farmyard fowl, as part of the fundamental process of socialisation that saw humankind move away from nomadic herding to settled farming. The remains of domestic web-footed fowl discovered among the grave goods in certain prehistoric burial sites in central northern Europe date from the Neolithic period. Mural decorations at Nineveh, in Mesopotamia, and at Saqqara and Giza, in Egypt, bear witness to the rearing of geese for ritual purposes. In Egypt, wall paintings dating as early as the 5th Dynasty show the practice of force-feeding by methods not unlike those used in traditional societies until some 50 years ago. This suggests that as long ago as 2800 BC there were those who knew how to appreciate the qualities of *foie gras*.

It was during this period that the goose became a sort of divine mother of humanity, the hypostasis of the soul of the pharaoh, a winged messenger (which in Christianity became an angel) linking the gods to humankind and, through the medium of ritual sacrifice, humankind to the gods. It was a bridge thrown across the divide between mortal existence and eternal life. It is no surprise, then, that the ancient Egyptians themselves gave the goose, as well as various other animals, a role of some importance in the rituals of birth and death, and it appears very likely that

TYPES OF GEESE		
Meat and liver	**Low-fat meat**	**Meat and feather**
Bourbon	Common goose	White Poitou goose
Emden	Alsace goose	Romagna goose
Tolosa	White Piacenza goose	
Pomeranian	Gray Padua goose	
Touraine	Normandy goose	
Gray Landes goose		

the privileged gastronomic relationship between the Jewish people and our particular fowl developed during the long period when "Israel dwelt in Egypt" and during the subsequent Exodus to the Promised Land. It is thought that the slaves entrusted with the task of rearing geese for the pharaoh, his family and the priesthood were Jewish, and that these same specialist goose herds took their skills with them to Palestine, where they taught their own people to appreciate the bird. Its characteristics also comply perfectly with the requirements of religious law and are therefore in keeping with kosher orthodoxy (the laws governing the purity of food). The Diaspora would then have spread this tradition to the four corners of the world.

In the Greek world, too, authors such as Homer, Eubulus, Epigenes, Aristotle, Atheneus and Plutarch all sang the praises of this useful bird, particularly when roasted; they appreciated not only its liver (considered to be the seat of the soul in esoteric culture) but also its docile nature and that particular, ineffable "philosophical wisdom" that rendered the goose so dear to their hearts.

FROM ROME TO THE MIDDLE AGES

Ancient Roman authors and naturalists such as Cato, Varro, Columella and Palladio welcomed the Greek heritage into Latin culture and set down a complete, codified system for rearing and fattening geese.

Contrary to Pliny's assertions, the goose was already held in high regard at this time not only for its meat and *foie gras* but also for its down and its fat, which was prized both in the kitchen and for cosmetic uses. Goose fat was used to concoct medicinal pomades and unguents to firm the breasts after childbirth or to tone and cleanse the skin. The reputation that

geese enjoyed – and in which many writers including Pliny himself believed – as excellent guardians to watch over the home or military posts is not confirmed by their ethology; it was probably nothing more than an attempt to find an explanation, couched in mythical terms (those of the Capitoline geese), for the ancient rituals, still dedicated to Juno in the Augustine period, whose original social motivation had been long forgotten.

Little information has been collated on the cooking and preparation of the goose in ancient times, but it can be assumed that it was prepared in the same manner as other web-footed fowl, such as swans, coots and ducks, which were usually roasted or boiled and covered in sauces made with spices and herbs, especially lovage.

Rearing geese was by no means confined to the Romans, however. Those peoples whom the Romans considered to be barbarians also fattened many a fine goose and the Romans themselves obtained supplies of geese from the Germanic tribes. That the art of fattening geese did not die out after the fall of the Roman Empire is due to the fact that this was already a well-known and profitably practiced activity among the nomadic peoples of central northern Europe. The Salic Law laid down by the Franks in the 8th century called for the remarkably large fine of 120 denarii as compensation for the theft of a goose, and specific regulations for their protection were laid down by Charlemagne in the early 9th century.

During the Middle Ages goose meat was sought after for salting, very much like pork, while the fat was used for preserving food. Quite spontaneously, in the widespread religious syncretism of the rural world, many pagan rites based on the sacrifice of the goose were adopted by Christianity. The end-of-harvest rituals still practised in south-western France and in vast areas of Umbria and the Marches in Italy were incorporated into Christian culture by means of association with St. Martin and the ritual eating of goose in memory of the bishop of Tours. This ritual is still practiced throughout continental Europe on November 11, just as the geese are passing overhead on their southerly migration.

MODERN GEESE

Although the goose was held in high regard by all the great chefs of the Renaissance, from Maestro Martino to Platina and from Messisbugo to the Scappi, goose rearing in Italy remained more or less confined to a cottage industry. In France, on the other hand, several sovereigns introduced legislation to ensure and protect the rearing of high-quality birds; in 1509 Louis XII signed the first patents granted to goose farmers that accorded them certain privileges in comparison with mere poultry farmers. Francis I, Henry II, Charles IX and many other monarchs up to Louis XVI also passed laws designed to ensure that France would always be kept well stocked with geese. Between 1782 and 1873, nevertheless, Louis XIV's parliament issued warrants for the arrest of three farmers because the excrement produced by their geese was rendering pasture unfit for use by

other animals. If these were the first signs of the Revolution of 1789 then they certainly did not lead to much; the innovations that enabled the production of *foie gras* to be carried out on an industrial scale, with rationalized, controlled production systems, were introduced to goose farming at the end of the 18th century, particularly in France and in Bohemia, then part of the kingdom of Hungary, where goose fattening was a famous tradition in the Jewish communities. In the space of a few years, the millet formerly used for fattening the geese was replaced with maize, selective breeding produced giant and more easily fattened strains of birds, and a funnel equipped with a piston was invented in order to cram the geese practically and quickly.

During the same period, the pie and pastry makers of Strasbourg, Toulouse and Périgueux emerged supreme in the production of goose *pâté de foie* and the typical characteristics that define the product were gradually established; the addition of liver from birds other than the goose was banned, and about a century later this process of definition reached the point where the characteristics of *foie gras* were given legal recognition thanks to the anti-fraud legislation passed by the French parliament in 1901 in which it was stipulated that "*foie gras* preserves must be prepared exclusively with goose and duck liver of excellent quality". With the gradual disappearance of traditional Jewish communities from 20th-century Europe, and the spread of poultry farming based on chicken and turkey in response to the rising demand from the population of the industrialized countries for meat from the fillet parts of the bird, goose farming has been drastically reduced in many regions of Europe and in some it has completely disappeared. The tradition of cooking with goose has always remained alive in France, thanks precisely to French *foie gras* production, and only recently have the bird's usefulness and potential begun to be rediscovered in some regions of Italy such as Veneto, Friuli, Lomellina, the Po region to the west of the Ticino, between Vercelli and Novara, and a few areas in Emilia Romagna and in Tuscany that had already been famous once before, at least until the beginning of the 20th-century, as goose-farming areas.

THE GOOSE IN ITALY, VENETO AND FRIULI

From 1980 to 1990, after a period of some 40 years in which goose farming sank into oblivion, and the goose's cackling and uncertain gait was no more than the stuff of distant memories or of arcadian whimsy on the pages of primary school reading books, the industrial viability of the goose was re-evaluated in Italy. In Morsano in Tagliamento, in Lower Friuli around Aquileia, in Viscone in the countryside around Palmanova as in other centers of southern Friuli, which is full of lakes and boggy areas, and in Veneto around Portogruaro, a few courageous entrepreneurs took the initiative and, not hesitating to give the cultural value of attachment to rural history its due, successfully reintroduced goose farming. From salting meat to creative gastronomy, from charcuterie to the not-so-diet-conscious crackling and *foie gras*, nothing has been forgotten of a culinary culture that only a few decades ago had been given up for lost. The most highly prized

of geese had in fact been fattened ever since Roman times in this frontier region, so close both to Slavic and Central European cultures, following a tradition that survived both barbarian raids and neglect during countless periods of foreign dominance. In the Joppi di Udine Municipal Library is a 14th-century manuscript with a cartoon-like ink drawing that depicts an everyday scene of mediaeval life (see page 42): a certain prelate Martin is shown presenting two geese to the patriarch Raimondo della Torre, who declares himself well pleased to receive them, uttering the phrase "Good is the goose".

Geese were valued in those uncertain times, as were wine, wheat, cheese and other foodstuffs that lent themselves to long

Foto: F. Mesturini

Goose farming in Lomellina culminates in the production of a unique local salami.

preservation, as a substantial part of the annual tax burden that communes or city-states paid to feudal lords and to the parochial church authorities. Those raised in the northeast were geese of a particular species native to Friuli, now almost disappeared, with characteristics similar to those of the Toulouse goose: of medium size, with white plumage flecked with gray, and capable of reaching weights of over 24 lb/11 kg after fattening.

Today this species survives only in southwestern France, in a triangular area lying between Bordeaux and the Pyrenees to which it was introduced by immigrants from Friuli at the beginning of the 20th century.

The strain that is known today as the Friuli goose is in fact the result of recent cross-breeding between the Emden and Romagna varieties: all the annual fairs and festivals that draw the attention of a growing public to goose farming and cuisine are no more than the most obvious sign of the new trend in the raising and farming of fowl in Italy.

LOMELLINA AND THE BORDERS OF PIEDMONT

The specialty in Friuli is cured goose "ham", which enthusiasts regard as a great delicacy if properly prepared and cured. The geese reared in Lomellina, on the other hand, are destined for the most part for the production of a celebrated goose salami. Lomellina is an area rich in marshland, irrigated meadows and

These geese play the leading role on posters and postcards marking the annual goose salami festival.

Portogruaro is goose country, and hosts a very popular goose fair each year.

springs. It boasts a centuries-old tradition of goose farming, which has never completely died out, but production is currently slightly down on recent decades – quite the reverse of the trend observed in other regions of Italy.

It is thought that geese-rearing in Lomellina dates back to remote times, as in the area of Piedmont to the west of Ticino and especially the Novarese region which was once part of the dominions of Milan. It was the influence of the Sforzas, dukes of Milan who were familiar with the lands of Mortara and Vigevano thanks to their passion for hunting, that encouraged the development of goose farming in this part of the country. It flourished easily here, partly thanks to the presence of a large Jewish community and partly because the goose was better suited than the pig to the Lomellina countryside.

In the past goose farming became so important in the local economy that in 1833 the town council of Rosasco, a Medieval borough to the south of Palestro, instituted the office of communal goose-warden, the holder of which had the specific duty of looking after the vast numbers of geese belonging to all the goose farmers in the commune (whose care was generally entrusted to less than watchful children). The communal warden had a contractual duty to herd all the geese out to pasture each day and restore them each evening to their legitimate owners, but above all to prevent them from causing damage to crops and sown fields during the day.

New strains were introduced into Lomellina during the 1960s, such as the swan goose (males) and the Romagna goose (females) but as in Friuli the most important factor in the creation of the strain known today as the Lomellina goose was cross-breeding between the local strain and the Emden goose. Thanks to this hybridization breeders have produced fowl of medium size capable of reaching a typical weight of 17½ lb/8 kg for the male and 14 lb/6.5 kg for the female in the space of four to five months; these birds are particularly well-suited to current market demand.

THE GOOSE AND THE JEWISH COMMUNITY

Hundreds of pages have been written, often in rather colorful vein, on the close links between the goose and the Jewish world in which our web-footed friend has undoubtedly played a role similar to that of the pig in Christian culture.

Documents preserved in the archives of many European cities bear witness to the fact that throughout the Middle Ages, and in some cases right up until the end of the 19th century, the most important goose farmers and the best known purveyors of meat and other products derived from geese that lived in the Jewish ghettos.

Some authorities argue that foie gras, goose charcuterie and, in the area to the north of the Po, goose cassoulet all originated in Jewish culture, though these assertions are often undocumented, based rather on induction and inspired more by a folkloristic instinct than by any attachment to historical truth; it can nevertheless be said that by the late Middle Ages and during the Renaissance these dishes were being prepared, with minor variations, in the Jewish ghettos of France, Hungary, Italy, and Germany. Non-Jewish cuisine of the same period was also undergoing a similar process of internationalization and the recipes of the late Medieval period – no matter which part of Europe they came from – all drew upon a single great supra-national cuisine with common features that were easy to translate from one locality to another. In his *Grande histoire du foie gras*, Silvano Serventi correctly concludes that the available historical documents strongly suggest that during the centuries before *foie gras* production was subject to its own legislation and became regulated, in France as in Hungary and throughout Europe in general, the Jewish communities were indeed the only ones who knew the secret of fattening geese for *foie gras*; this is not to say that they were the only ones fattening geese, but that they fattened them better than others could do. The dish that the French began to know as *foie gras* in the sixteenth century was merely called *fegato* (liver) in Italy and *Leber* (liver) in Germany, but was essentially the same product; it is still found today, together with the pâté made from it, in the Jewish cuisine of Novara, Mantua, Veneto, Trieste, Livorno and Rome.

As for the famous *cassoeula*, or cassoulet, the question of whose origins is the subject of an age-old controversy, there is no doubt that the earliest systematic references to this dish, which come from non-Jewish sources, define a pottage of mixed vegetables and fowl. Between the early 18th century and the end of the 19th century, the use of fowl gradually replaced pork until eventually goose cassoulet became a separate dish in its own right. This was not, then, exclusive to Jewish kosher cuisine, though perfectly suited to it.

JEWISH CULTURE AND CHARCUTERIE

In accordance with ancient tradition, in the days leading up to *Pesach*, or Passover, the purveyors of kosher foods in those cities where there is still an established Jewish community sell goose charcuterie produced in accordance with the religious laws on food purity. These dishes, which for the most part are homemade, must be prepared using meat that has been thoroughly bled and not mixed with any other impure meat. The preparation of products intended for sale is often overseen by the community's rabbi, who marks every single item with a seal to certify it kosher.

Goose salami is a typical Italian product, whether it is stuffed in the traditional way using the skin of the bird's own neck as the casing or in the more modern way, using casing made of lambs' or calves' intestines; it is unknown among the Jewish communities of the rest of Europe and even in Israel, where salami is made exclusively from beef. Cured "hams", salty goose crackling and goose *sovrane* (goose sovereigns, goose "supreme" consisting of salted and cured breast meat still in its skin like a spotless bresaola) are however, like *pâté de foie*, known and produced by Jewish people in almost every country of Europe, although in limited quantities mainly intended for family consumption and using techniques influenced by the various different national cuisines.

Even in areas where there is a strong Jewish presence, and despite the fact that these products derive from the ancient culture of the ghetto, most of the goose charcuterie available on the market, such as *Mortara salami* (which has to be cooked before is can be eaten) and *cacciatorini* (small sausages) or the Friuli salami and goose sausage, is now made with the addition of large amounts of non-kosher or even forbidden meats, such as pork, and are therefore excluded from the Jewish tradition.

THE REARING OF GEESE

Geese reared for meat

Whether geese are reared for meat, *foie gras* or goose down, the quality of the end product depends on care at every stage of the cycle. In order to obtain the finest geese, irrespective of the specific procedures adopted for raising them, the goose farmer must pay attention to every detail of their growth. To call the farming of geese a vocation, as some authors do, is perhaps an exaggeration but the uncompromising tone of the word gives a good idea of the level of commitment and devotion required to

make goose farming profitable; such devotion is captured in any number of traditional oleographs, printed in imitation of oil paintings, depicting the figure of a doting goose-girl with her eternal cackling, feathery flock trailing behind her.

A "roasting" goose of the Friuli breed (an Emdén-Romagna cross) needs 11-12 weeks, or some 80 days, to reach its optimum weight for slaughter. The best results are obtained with geese allowed to live in the open in a semiwild state, on pastureland or in enclosures provided with shelter and mangers to supply them with green forage.

Geese are monogamous in the wild, but become polygamous when reared as farm birds. For maximum fertility levels, the ideal ratio is that of one male to every three females, but a ratio of 1:4, often used in practice, does not result in any significant reduction in fertility. Goose eggs hatch at 28-30 days, and for the first two weeks after hatching the goslings need to be housed at a temperature of 100°F/38°C. This is then gradually lowered until, when the chicks are about 20 days old, the temperature reaches 68°F/20°C. With suitable feeding, comprising ground meal of various types in the early weeks, the goslings rapidly gain weight. Within two months they are capable of multiplying

their weight no less than 45-fold.

In the past all geese were fattened in the same way in order to obtain the greatest possible quantity of meat and fat, which was needed in cooking both for flavoring and for preserving food. Current farming techniques, however, cater to the idea that a goose raised for meat should not have excessive quantities of fat so as to maximize its nutritional potential and its flavor, odor and texture. Thanks to modern methods, involving the use of incubators to hatch the eggs, seasonal production, which once limited consumption to the period between the feast of St Martin (November 11) and the New Year, is a thing of the past. Nowadays, producers market goose meat as a food for all seasons with a wide range of commercial prospects.

Geese reared for down and feathers

The Poitou white goose is prized as the best breed for feathers and skins, and, like all geese reared for their feathers, it enjoys a few more months of life than its meat-producing cousins. In the traditional May-to-December cycle of production these geese are allowed a life span of some 200 days, during which they are plucked four times at intervals of about 40 days. After slaughtering, the geese are plucked for a fifth and last time, while still warm. Those geese that hatch early, in February, are plucked one more time than the rest. During the course of its fairly short existence, a single goose can produce up to 1½ lb/600 g of feathers (not counting the soft downy skin of the neck, the abdomen and the wings). This is not a very large amount, which explains the high cost of clothing and of items such as duvets and quilted jackets that contain pure goose down. The practise of plucking the animals alive, though apparently cruel, is in fact perfectly suited to the life cycle of a bird of Nordic origin that has some difficulty adapting to a temperate climate.

The goose as weed controller

An animal of insatiable appetite, the goose has recently begun to attract attention as being useful in organic and biodynamic farming. Taking advantage of the selective feeding habits of geese, some farmers in the United States, and in the last few years in southern Italy, are experimenting with the use of geese on farmland planted with crops – such as potato, sugarcane, cotton, maize, and orchard fruits – that geese will not touch. A dozen geese grazing between the rows of a crop are capable of carrying out, without the use of herbicides, a task that it would normally take one farm worker to do: they keep the crop free of weeds and even thoroughly hoe the ground with their beaks. At present this use of geese is no more than experimental, but it is clear that some potential lies in the rational exploitation of the interaction between an animal and the environment in which it lives.

Geese reared for foie gras

Geese intended for *foie gras* production are reared in a production cycle centered around a life span of about six months, traditionally ending with the slaughter in October of geese hatched between April and May. Modern rearing methods, however, are no longer closely bound to the passage of the seasons. Once the bird's body structure has developed and the goose has fattened naturally on green forage, producers move on to the cramming phase that induces rapid weight gain, especially in its liver; force-feeding causes the infiltration of large quantities of fatty tissue into the cells of the liver.

In centuries gone by geese were crammed using a special funnel provided with a wooden dowel to force the food into the bird's esophagus. The ancient Romans used to cram geese with fresh or dried figs, sometimes mixed with other calorie-rich foodstuffs such as nuts; the Egyptians and Greeks used ground meal or bran mixed into a paste with water. During the Middle Ages producers generally used mixtures of various grains, more or less finely ground, to which fruit was often added.

Up to the end of the 19th century, when the practice was forbidden by law, some producers, like those in the Jewish ghettos of Hungary and France, would add to this mash such toxic substances as antimony, which appears to make the liver particularly large and tender. In some case producers hobbled the birds and kept them in darkness prevent them from moving

and encourage weight-gain by restricting their usual expenditure of energy.

Fattening

In modern goose farming cramming is fully automated and, the producers assure us, does not cause the bird pain if carried out with due care. For the cramming stage to be successful it has to be preceded by a pre-cramming period when the birds are fed with large amounts of greenery and roots so that their stomach and viscera become large enough to hold large quantities of food.

The mash most commonly used for cramming is made up of ground and boiled maize mixed with fat as a lubricant in a proportion of 1 oz per 2 lb/25g per 1 kg, with salt in a proportion of ⅓-½ oz per 2 lb/10-15g per 1 kg and sometimes with milk enzymes to regulate the functioning of the intestines. White or yellow maize is used depending on whether the producer wishes to give the *foie gras* a pink or an ocher-gray color. During cramming a goose takes in 44-55 lb/20-25 kg of mash and its liver can reach a weight of 1 lb-1 lb 14 oz/500-900 g.

The ethical problem of whether it is legitimate to cram geese in order to enlarge their livers is not easy to resolve. The defenders of animal rights are ranked on one side, arguing that cramming is a barbaric and cruel practice that causes deformities and suffering in the animal; on the other, *foie gras* producers and consumers retort that a crammed goose, although fat, is a healthy animal with a healthy liver that is capable, should cramming cease and the goose not be slaughtered, of returning rapidly to its original weight and shape with no signs of cirrhosis of the liver or cancer of the esophagus. The issue cannot be avoided: but this is not a dispute that can be resolved here.

GOOSE PRESERVES

Prosciuttino – cured goose "hams"

Highly appreciated in the goose farming regions of Italy, goose charcuterie is almost unknown to the general public outside these fortunate areas. Gourmets regard it as the very finest of all the non-pork-based charcuterie, so exquisitely do its flavors combine; far from the hefty, bold attractions of pork charcuterie, these goose-meat creations are as delicately flavored as if they still had in them something of a feather's lightness. The king of this anserine court is undoubtedly the *prosciuttino*, or cured goose "ham", the delicate refined baby brother of the great but more obtrusive pork ham – rather like the tiny youngest son of traditional fairy tales.

These "hams" have been prepared since the late Middle Ages, especially in Friuli, Lomellina, and in the region around Novara. Depending on the producer, they may be on or off the bone, single or double (two thighs wrapped in a single strip of skin) like those of San Daniele, flavored with spices and aromatic plants from the kitchen garden, or lightly smoked, but in practice they are all made following fairly similar procedures.

After plucking and cleaning, the thighs are removed from the bird together with the meat around them. The thighs are rubbed with saltpeter, sprinkled with salt and pepper and allowed to stand, completely buried in coarse salt for about two weeks, often with a weight on top so that the meat loses all its liquid. After this period, the skin has to be sewn back around the meat and the "hams" are salted and spiced; they can then be hung in a cool place for the necessary curing. In traditional farmhouse-style preparation curing never takes less than two months, but with ventilated curing the time taken can be almost halved. Using a similar procedure to that followed to make cured goose "hams", producers in Friuli and Mortara also make the so-called *sovrane* ("sovereigns"); these consists of a couple of goose breasts, rather than thighs, that are sewn into their own skin and left to cure for some two months, sometimes after being briefly smoked.

Charcuterie

Now that goose farming has been rationalized and is no longer tied to the bird's biological cycle, goose meat can be produced all year round. Whereas previously no such choice existed, it is now possible to make a careful selection of the meat to be sent for charcuterie. To the advantage of producers, there is much scope for long-life products such as cured goose "hams" and other goose charcuterie to win the appreciation they deserve – all the more so since the merit and high quality of these delicacies should lead them to be marketed well beyond the confines of the area in which they are produced.

A great variety of salamis are made, ranging from those containing goose meat and goose fat alone, which are derived directly from Jewish culture, to those mixed to a greater or lesser extent with pork and pork fat, and from those stuffed into a casing made from the skin of the goose's neck to those made in an industrial manner and stuffed into casings made of the common pig intestines, whether coarse-grained or finely ground.

All are products of the greatest refinement, the fruit of a centuries-old process of preparation, offering the gourmet the chance to experience a stunning taste of savors and aromas.

As in the case of pork salamis, the taste and aroma of goose salamis varies from one producer to another since individual producers use the ingredients in different proportions, different quantities and selections of spices (garlic, pepper, fennel and nutmeg are the most common), and add their own personal touches (the mixture may be enriched with a drop of oil or the addition of white wine). Goose salamis are generally eaten raw. The exception is the Mortara salami, which must be cooked before it reaches the table, and is served cold and sliced by hand like the usual liver *mortadella*.

Another particularly celebrated type of salami, produced in the area between Padua and Novara, is the *salam d'la duja* (potted salami), a small salami only slightly dried and stored for several months under fat. It is then used whenever required, sliced and grilled as the perfect accompaniment to a steaming mound of thick polenta.

There are also several different types of sausage. The long, Lugano-style sausage made with similar mixtures and seasonings to those of the salamis is also eaten with polenta or, after the custom in regions influenced by Middle European culture, as an accompaniment to boiled potatoes and cooked vegetables.

Goose crackling

In the past, it was common practice in rural societies to store a great variety of foods in a *duja*, or covered terracotta container. Certain gastronomical collections compiled during the 19th century record recipes (reproduced as curiosities in more recent books) for preserving goose meat by following an ancient and universal procedure that, in the days when refrigeration and vacuum-packing were unknown, made it possible to preserve meat over long periods as if it had only just been slaughtered and cooked. The meat was lightly salted, cut into fairly small pieces, and allowed to hang in a cool place for a couple of days to drain. Once drained dry, the meat was cooked in goose fat and then placed in a *duja*: the fat it had been cooked in was thoroughly filtered, and then used to cover the meat completely.

As already mentioned, salamis could be stored by following a similar procedure, as could goose livers wrapped in lamb's caul. This is a Medieval specialty that has been completely forgotten today except in regions of central Italy; everywhere else it has been swept into oblivion by the irresistible rise of the noble *foie gras* and its pâté. Meat could even be preserved in this way for as long as eight to nine months, from the fall until the beginning of the following summer; for societies tied to consuming only what they themselves could produce, this was a unique supply of protein.

The fat used in the kitchen for cooking and in the pantry for preserving was obtained by cooking the fatty tissues and skin of the goose over an extremely low heat (or in a double boiler). The skin itself was used to make crackling, or *graton* as it was known in Lomellina, an hors d'œuvre that is delicious eaten hot but that is also extremely good cold and capable of keeping for quite some time; it is one of those rustic specialties that was once the delight of tables that were strangers to more lordly splendors. Little scraps of skin left over from the preparation of grander dishes were cooked for an interminable time over an imperceptibly low heat until they lost all their fat and became dry and crunchy – a tidbit well worthy of being taken on board the Ark, should there ever be a second Noah entrusted with saving all that can be saved.

FOIE GRAS

The rhetoric of gastronomy undoubtedly reaches its climax in many thousands of pages devoted throughout the world to *foie gras*: the periodic ritual exaltation of the tastebuds is transformed into a universal myth, into the symbol of the utmost heights that food can reach not only for those who, like the French, consider it to be their very own irresistible peccadillo but also for those who are not familiar with eating it at all. For all that, it is difficult to talk in terms of myth, it is only too easy to become carried away, whether in enthusiastic praise or blasphemous railing. So perhaps it is to keep to the facts, leaving aside the poetry of words and always remembering that *foie gras* is no more than a food – no matter how unique it is thought to be.

Foie gras, then, the liver of a goose or duck fattened by cramming, is a gastronomic specialty that has been known for some thousands of years in the countries of the Mediterranean, in northern Europe, and in the Far East, but which in its current form is essentially a modern creation. The French are both the largest producers (providing 60 per cent of the world market) and the most enthusiastic consumers of *foie gras*, and it is they who have established its characteristics and regulated production over the last two centuries by passing a succession of laws. Other countries that account for a significant share of the market (Hungary, Israel, the former Yugoslavia, Bulgaria, and Poland) have substantially adapted their production to conform to French legislation, partly because French gastronomy retains its ascendancy over international haute cuisine.

Dishes using *foie gras* and *pâté de foie* have long been widely known in the traditional culture of many countries, including Italy, but it is undeniable that the specialties that are celebrated everywhere – such as *foie gras en croûte* and *foie gras* in aspic, the various mousses and *pâté en terrine*, grilled medallions and

escalopes of *foie gras* with truffles – all originated in France, and that together they constitute both the pride of French cuisine but also, as Jean François Revel has emphasized, the limitation of a gastronomy with an inherent tendency to be inward-looking.

Historical notes

In *De re coquinaria* Apicius laconically refers to goose liver as *ficatum*, taking the fact that it was fat liver for granted. The term is in fact a contraction of *iecur ficatum*, liver fattened with figs. This was the technique used by the ancient Romans to cause the goose's liver to increase in size while improving its flavor. It is worth noting that goose liver was so highly prized that it led to the Latin term *iecur* being dropped from the language during the late Roman Empire, the adjective *ficatum* becoming a noun. From *ficatum* is derived the modern Italian *fegato* (liver), the common term used to describe the hepatic gland of any animal. Almost all the Medieval recipe books contain references, however vague, to fat liver; but in the mid-17th century Vincenzo Tanara wrote with reference to the goose in his *Economia del cittadino in villa* (*The Citizen's Household Management*) that "the liver is cooked in all the manners of other livers ... and with all the more success for it is the tenderest of them all". This is rather a general judgement but one that points the way toward what was to follow during the course of the next three centuries.

Some French authors continue to attribute the first modern, systematic rules for the basic *foie gras* recipe (that is, subsequent to those set down by Apicius) to the *Opera dell'arte del cucinare* (*Work of the Art of Cooking*) of 1570 by Bartolomeo Scappi, cook to Pius V. They have failed to notice, however, that Scappi's recipe is nothing more than yet another variant on the recipes for liver wrapped in lamb's caul or pig's caul that appeared in half of the European recipe books from the year 300 onward. Furthermore, the first credible systematic rules for a *pâté de foie gras* are hidden away in one of these very recipe books, compiled by an anonymous Tuscan author of the 14th century, who wrote: "and if [the gosling] be not fat, put it inside bacon fat ... and with the liver roasted and pounded with the said breadcrumb: and all things soaked in vinegar, make it to boil and put into it pepper, saffron, cloves and other good spices." It is a pity that, in the usual Medieval fashion, our anonymous cook merely refers to this thick paste by the term *peverada* (peppered paste).

Another pâté is hinted at in the famous *Kochbuch* (*Cookbook*) printed in Frankfurt in 1581, which speaks of a purée obtained from a goose's liver weighing more than 3 lb (almost 1.5 kg). The actual term *foie gras*, however, was recorded for the first time in the treatise *Le cuisinier français* (*The French Cook*) of 1651 by Pierre François La Varenne: and so French gastronomic culture staked its claim to the product.

Categories of foie gras

For the French, *foie gras* is an affair of state. Everyone must know where to find the best, how to choose it, how to store it, how to cook it and (nor could it be otherwise, considering that we are dealing here with a national legend) how best to serve it. In France, *foie gras* is available raw, fresh, semicooked and canned. Raw *foie gras* is intended for professional chefs and for those gourmets with the necessary skills to cook or process it. The *foie gras* should be very firm when bought, not too fatty, weighing between 14 oz and 1 lb 8 oz (400-700 g), and of an even pinkish-beige color tending toward yellow. This is the least expensive way to buy *foie gras*, and when vacuum-packed and refrigerated it can be kept for up to a week.

Fresh *foie gras*, unlike the raw form, has already been prepared by the producer: it will have been cleaned, seasoned and cooked for 7-8 minutes at 176°F (80°C). This form best retains all the nuances of aroma and taste. Vacuum-cooking, which has been used for some 15 years, represents a minor revolution in the preparation of fresh *foie gras*; this method extracts only a small proportion of the fat and retains the rich aroma perfectly intact. *Foie gras* in this form can be kept in the refrigerator for up to two weeks.

Semi-cooked *foie gras* is slightly more cooked than fresh *foie gras* but less cooked than the canned product. This method, which has been in use for only about a quarter of a century, makes it possible to market *foie gras* all year round. Semi-cooked *foie gras* is available in jars, in cans, or vacuum-packed, and can be kept in the refrigerator for up to six months.

Canned *foie gras* is the ancestor of all other forms of *foie gras*, and until the beginning of this century it represented practically the entire market. It is cooked for a longer time and at a higher temperature than the other types of *foie gras* in order to achieve complete sterilization.

An unopened and undamaged can, correctly stored in a cellar that is not too damp, may be kept for well over the four years laid down in French law. French gourmets maintain that *foie gras*, like a fine wine, improves when laid down and aged; it is left for longer so that it can slowly reabsorb some of the fat removed during cooking.

Of the great variety of products derived from *foie gras*, the most common are *pâté* and *purée*. By law, *pâté de foie gras* must contain at least 50 per cent *foie gras*, and *purée* at least 20 per cent. The law permits these derivative products to be larded, covered with stuffings of various kinds or with aspic, or to have Armagnac, Port, Cognac or Périgord truffles added to them.

NUTRITIONAL VALUES

If consumption of goose meat and *foie gras* products gradually declined during the course of this century, at least until their rediscovery in recent years, this was due for the most part to a widespread prejudice against a foodstuff regarded as too fatty and therefore incompatible with the dietary canons of our age. Indeed, if an average figure is taken, goose meat has a nutritional value of close to 400 kcl per 3½ oz/100g, higher than that of chicken or turkey; only fatty pork is higher in calories. Taken in isolation, the lean meat of the goose (such as the breast or thigh), however, has a nutritional value ranging between 125 and 145 kcl per 3½ oz/100g. This is the same value as for chicken thigh, veal escalopes or lean pork chops.

It is quite another story when it comes to *foie gras*, however, which weighs in at 520 kcl per 3½ oz/100g, more than any other meat except cured sausage and pork crackling. However, because *foie gras* is an expensive delicacy, it is consumed in modest quantities, and it is richer in monounsaturated acids than in saturated and polyunsaturated acids. One authority assures that "there is no nutritional reason to forego of the pleasure of a good *foie gras* because of a dieting or for the sake of a balanced diet."

The prelate Martin presents two geese to the patriarch Raimondo della Torre, drawing in pen and ink from a 14th-century manuscript in the Joppi di Udine Municipal Library.

Some accounts of how goose was prepared in the cuisine of the past

ORTENSIO LANDO
Catalog of the things which are eaten and of the beverages which are used today.
PUBLISHED IN VENICE IN 1548

Alessandro Etholo, poet, was the first who ate of the goose, which by nature is of the warmest stomach, and therefore we see it desirous of herbs which are cold, and its thirst slaked with water: and although it be desirous of grazing upon herbs and various leafy fronds, yet does it never touch laurel. The heart of the goose is already praised among the most praised of foods. Scipio, or Metello, or Sessio, for it is among these three that the thing is disputed, was the first who fattened the livers with milk and with cooked wine, and who did eat of them.

ANTONIO FRUGOLI
Usage and Carving ...
PUBLISHED IN ROME IN 1631

Goose necks stuffed in various manners
The necks of the said geese may be stuffed with minced lean meat of the said geese, or with other minced meats, with barbaglia or prosciutto cut fine, with good herbs, and egg, with grated cheese inside, with enough spices, and sharp-tasting grapes in their season, or Muscat grapes without their pits, and they shall be served hot, after being cooked in meat broth, and they can be stuffed with yet other sundry stuffings also, and they shall be served as above.

GIOVANNI FRANCESCO VASSELLI
Apicius, or the Master of Banquets
PUBLISHED IN BOLOGNA IN 1647

Of the gizzards of the goose, and their lean flesh
The gizzards of the goose, after they are boiled, are finely sliced, and their lean flesh is chopped up very small, and of this "caprices" are made like the "caprices" made of beef by putting the slices of

gizzard around the edge of the plate, with sprigs of parsley or Roman mint, with half-crushed pepper, sprinkling it with clove vinegar. I cannot speak very highly of this animal, for I do not find it praised by the Medici nor by the ancients nor the moderns for its great moistness, and those which are reared in the house are the worse for they have but little exertion. I find no other good in them but the liver, which is most nourishing, of excellent savor, and has the power to reduce the flux caused by liver because of its weakness ...

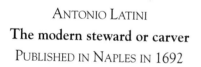

COMMENTARIO
DELLE PIV NOTABILI,
& moſtruoſe coſe d'Italia, & altri
luoghi : di lingua Aramea in
Italiana tradotto.

CON VN BREVE CATALOGO,
de gli inuentori delle coſe che ſi mangiano
& beueno, nouamente ritrouato.

IN VENETIA,
Appreſſo Giouanni Bariletto.
M. D. LXIX.

ANTONIO LATINI
The modern steward or carver
PUBLISHED IN NAPLES IN 1692

The goose can suit in all the dishes in which the duck suits, and be served with the very same condiments; the fat of it is usually set aside to condiment various dishes for it succeeds exceedingly well in all of them. Stuffed, like the ducks, it can

be cooked unseasoned and be served hot, covered with sundry pastes, herbs and salamis as has been said of the domestic ducks. It can be roasted in the oven, whole, with stuffing, being served hot. It can be done minced, or stewed, in pieces or in quarters, served hot, with aromatic herbs, suitable spices and other

well proportioned ingredients. It can be roasted, with stuffing, or without, larded, and served hot, with savor, as you will. It can be cooked on the coals, with Malmsey, roasted on the grill, in pieces, or in quarters, basted with liquified bacon, basted with vinegar, with its crust upon it, served hot, with sauce, or another savor, as you will. It can be cooked in a pie, or breaded, whole, in pieces, or in quarters, with the same condiments as the duck. The liver of the same can be put to steep in milk and of it there can be made sundry fried, and roasted dishes, in all the manners already said of the liver of veal, and of the domestic pig.

VINCENZO CORRADO
The Gallant Cook
PUBLISHED IN NAPLES IN 1786

Goose with spring onions
After the goose shall have been cleaned it shall be put to cook in a pot with prosciutto and aromatic herbs; and when

cooked it shall be served with spring onions tossed in butter.

Goose in the country style
The goose is stuffed with rice cooked in meat juices, and mixed with prosciutto, Parmesan, pork cervelat, and beef marrow; it shall be cooked in a closed stewpot, and it shall be served in its own juice.

The Piedmont Cook
Adapted to the Latest Taste
PUBLISHED IN MILAN IN 1805

Goose with mustard
Take a young and tender goose, pluck it, singe it, and draw it; cut out the liver which you will mix with two spring onions, half a head of garlic, parsley, and shallot all ground up, a bay leaf, pounded basil, and thyme ground to a powder, a good piece of butter, salt and ground pepper, stuff the goose with this, and once sewed up, cook it on the spit, basting it

from time to time with butter, and as you baste it, first put the dripping pan beneath so as not to lose what falls. When the goose shall be almost cooked, add a spoonful of mustard into the butter with which you have basted it, put this back on the goose and cover it all over with ground bread, finish cooking it and brown it, serving it with a sauce made in this wise. Put some butter in a saucepan with two handfuls of flour, a spoonful of mustard and a teaspoonful of vinegar, a

Aleſſandro Etholo poeta fu il primo che mãgiaſſe l'oca, la cui natura è di calidiſſimo ſtomaco, et perciò la ueggiamo uaga di herbe fredde, & dalle acque irri gate: & anchora che di paſcer herbe & uarie frondi uaga ſia, non tocca però mai l'alloro. Lodoſſi gia il cuor dell'oca fra i lodatiſſimi cibi. Scipione, o Metello, ouero Seſſio, che fra queſti tre batte la coſa, fu il primo che ingraſſaſſe i fegati con il latte, & con il uin cotto, & che ſe li mangiaſſe.

Extract from Catalog of the things which are eaten and of the beverages which are used today by Ortensio Lando, 1548. See page 43.

small glass of gravy or broth, salt and pepper, thicken it over the flame and serve it over the goose as an entrée.

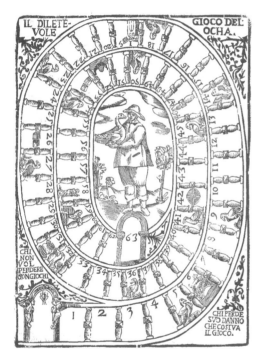

The game of "Goose", of Medieval or even more ancient origin, shows the importance of this animal in everyday life and also in the popular imagination.

Oniatology, or a discussion of foods with the recipes and rules for cooking correctly after the modern fashion
PUBLISHED IN FLORENCE IN 1806

A goose roasted after the English manner
Having first cleaned it well, and singed the goose, of which you will set aside the liver, prepare the following stuffing. Take ¾ cup/160 g of the white fat from veal kidneys, and clean it from the skin to mix it together with eight, or ten chicken livers as well as that of the said goose: chop the leaves of a bunch of sage, and an onion, and pound all these said foodstuffs, season with salt, pepper, ground cinnamon, and grated nutmeg, and stuff the goose with it. Cut off its neck, leaving the skin long, which you will sew at the back, so that the stuffing will not escape from where you removed the innards: cut off the wings, secure the thighs with a wooden skewer, wrap it, and in this manner put it to roast. It should turn for at least an hour and a half, after which you shall unwrap it, salt it and brown it handsomely. Arrange it in a dish with a little of the good cooking juices, removing the skewer: sew it up.

The sauce after the English manner should be made in the following way. Peel and core some lazzerole apples, cutting each of them into four parts, and put them in a saucepan covered with water, with the zest of a fresh lemon, hard cinnamon, and about ¼ cup/80 g of pergamena sugar: boil over a high flame, and when they are well cooked mash them with the ladle, and when you have drained the liquid add a piece of fresh butter: remove the lemon zest and the cinnamon so that the apple will blend with the butter. Pour this into a sauce boat and serve it at table together with the above mentioned roast.

FRANCESCO LEONARDI
The Modern Apicius
PUBLISHED IN ROME IN 1808

Goose pie

Bone the geese and lard the meat of these birds with lardons of bacon fat seasoned with salt, fine spices, and ground aromatic herbs, season the meat too with salt and fine spices; arrange it in the Pie with a finger or more of pounded bacon fat beneath it, and seasoned in the usual manner, a few truffles in the corners if you have them; cover with slices of bacon fat, pieces of butter, finish the pie, cook it for about six hours and serve it well browned, cold.

Goose after the English manner

Take a tender and plump goose, and singe it, remove the remains of the feathers, and draw it, stuff it with its liver pounded and seasoned with shallot, parsley, chives, truffles, a clove of garlic, all of this pounded, salt, crushed pepper, nutmeg, bacon slivers, a little butter, two raw egg yolks, sew it up, truss it with the legs skinned, and the toes clipped, folded back on the thighs, and roast it on the spit. When it is almost cooked sprinkle it with finely grated breadcrumbs, brown it, and serve it on a gravy made of beef with a little pounded shallot, salt, crushed pepper and the juice of a large lemon or of an orange.

Easy, Economical and Healthful Cuisine
PUBLISHED IN MILAN IN 1844

Salmis of goose

Take some roasted geese and cut them up small; make a roux and gently brown four spring onions in it. Put in a demijohn or a quarter of wine and as much again of broth, salt, pepper, selected herbs; boil the whole, then steep the pieces of goose in it and cook over a slow flame for half an hour: and at the moment of serving, thicken the gravy with a spoonful of oil and lemon juice: toast some slices of bread and arrange them around the dish. Put the pieces of goose in the middle and pour over the sauce.

FRANCESCO CHAPUSOT
PUBLISHED IN TURIN IN 1851

Roast goose

Take a fine goose, and when you have drawn it with care, and singed it, and cleaned it well inside, insert a little butter into the body with the minced zest of a lemon. Put it in a saucepan with enough butter and two cloves, and sprinkle it with fine salt; cover the saucepan well, and put it so that the heat is below and above, but not too strong, leave it to fry for two hours at least, and turn it from time to time. A little before serving it, remove the fat and instead of it add a few spoonfuls of water. Boil for a moment longer, then arrange your roast on a dish and pour the juices over it.

You can mix a little mustard and the sour juice of a lemon with the gravy.

GIAMBATTISTA BASEGGIO
Celius Apicius, of Victuals and Condiments, or of the Culinary Art
PUBLISHED IN VENICE IN 1852

Hot boiled goose with cold Apician sauce
Mince up pepper, lovage, coriander, mint, rue; season and mix with a little oil. Dry the boiled goose, still boiling hot, with a clean dishcloth; pour the sauce over it and put on the table.

GIOVANNI FELICE LURASCHI
The New Economical Milanese Cook
PUBLISHED IN MILAN IN 1853

Goose liver after the manner of the House of Stuart
This dish may be made during carnival or also at the beginning of the fall and during Christmas. Take three or four goose livers, carefully remove all of the gall, put them in milk and leave them there for a day, then take them out of the milk, cook them in braising juices simmering very gently, leave them to cook for half an hour and more, take them out of the cooking juices, remove the fat from the juices and reduce them, pile the livers on a dish and pour their juices over them, scatter with croutons (optional) and serve them. This dish can be served in a pan made of silver or of another compound which is like silver, as is presently the custom.

The Milanese Cook and the Piedmont Cook
PUBLISHED IN MILAN IN 1859

Goose with chestnuts on the spit
Peel a great many chestnuts, fry them for a moment in butter so as to remove their second skin more easily, then chop them together with the goose liver, add some chopped sausage meat, bacon rind, garlic, parsley, onions chopped extremely fine, salt, pepper, and nutmeg, cook this stuffing on the fire for a moment, then stuff the goose with it,

French gourmets maintain that canned foie gras improves with age and that if it to be enjoyed at its best it should be laid down.

sew it up again and put it on the spit and cook it.

GIOVANNI VIALARDI
Simple and Economic Bourgeois Cooking
PUBLISHED IN TURIN IN 1863

Stuffed goose after the fashion of Novara
Mince three hectograms (10 oz/300g) of haunch of veal without nerves, two hectograms (7 oz/200 g) of bacon, an onion, a little garlic, parsley, salt, pepper, and spices, all very fine; mix with it a hectogram (½ cup/100 g) of rice; take a well cleaned goose, fill it with the above mentioned stuffing, clean it and cook it in the same manner, but without wine; when cooked until tender, carve it and serve it with a good risotto made with its cooking juices.

CATERINA PRATO
A cookery manual for beginners and for experienced cooks
PUBLISHED IN GRAZ IN 1892

Roast goose
Take a goose thoroughly cleaned and prepared, salt it well, particularly inside, and rub the whole with marjoram, pepper or also with ground cumin.

The stomach may be filled with diced boiled potatoes or with peeled roast chestnuts or also with macaroni broken up very fine and boiled. Put it on the spit and secure it well, roast it slowly, basting it frequently with broth and butter, then with the juices that drip from it. Remove the excess fat from the dripping-pan placed beneath it before it becomes brown.

For cooking young geese three quarters of an hour is enough, while for those that are older and fatter, which should be stewed somewhat before roasting, two hours are needed. The roast goose is garnished with its own stuffing or it

is served with fruit compôte or stewed radish (horseradish) made with almonds.

GIOVANNI NELLI
The King of Cooks: a Treatise on Universal Gastronomy
PUBLISHED IN MILAN IN 1898

Goose in the country style
Take a fat white goose; remove the wings and prepare it in the usual way; mince the liver, adding some other to it; dice three large onions, toss them in butter and cook them unseasoned; add a pinch of ground sage, the liver, salt, and pepper; stuff the goose with this mixture; sew it up and truss it keeping the legs stretched out, having cut off the nails; cook it on the spit, arrange it on a dish and serve it with beef gravy or white veal, reduced.

Basic preparation and recipes

GERMANO PONTONI

CARVING GOOSE

1. CARVING WHEN RAW

Make a clean cut along the backbone with the tip of a carving knife, starting beside the wishbone. This is subsequently removed by cutting from the other side too. Open out slightly with the hands, and then cut the breast firmly in half along the sternum: this gives the two goose breasts. Pull the thighs apart slightly and cut through the joint.

The breast should finally be carved into three to four pieces starting with the wing joint with a little of the breast attached and continuing toward the sternum, carving with the knife at a slight angle. Generally speaking, however, the breast is not used in stewed goose dishes because prolonged cooking in a stew would render the breast meat stringy and tough. The thigh is cut in half and then into quarters.

Goose is available on the market ready-jointed with whole breasts. Goose thighs are also available vacuum-packed.

2. CARVING WHEN COOKED

Goose is usually carved as a roast. Start by carefully removing the wings, locating the joint and cutting through it with a strong carving knife. Then make a cut in the skin of the lower abdomen around the thighs, pull the thigh slightly away from the body with the aid of a carving fork and cut through the thigh joint which joins it to the body, removing it cleanly.

The two thighs are then each carved into at least three pieces, one of which corresponds to the shank while the other two are cut from the thigh proper.

The breast is sliced with a sharp knife, cutting vertically right down to the carcass, and it must be carved with care so that its shape can be reassembled on the serving dish. If you wish to serve the breast with part of the sternum, make a cut in the middle of the breast first with a very sharp carving knife and ending by striking the bone sharply. Then proceed as for the other manner of carving.

HOW TO REMOVE THE BREAST

Cut the tendon located behind the wing with a sharp knife. Cut from here to the middle of the back, boning the breast by sliding the knife in between the ribs and the meat until you reach the sternum, the bone which holds the whole breast together. It is important to bone and divide the breast with all its skin on because this can be used in the preparation of subsequent dishes (such as stuffing) and it protects the meat during cooking, preventing it from drying out too much. The sternum is sometimes left attached to the breast.

HOW TO BONE THE CARCASS

1. FROM THE NECK

This is the classic professional method that is used in order to stuff the goose as if it were a bag. The bones and entrails are removed through the neck opening. The goose is first thoroughly cleaned and any remaining feathers are singed off, after which a longitudinal cut is made starting from just below the neck and ending above the neck. This cut is opened a little wider, and the neck bone is removed first using a very sharp knife. Then, taking care not to cut the skin, the person dressing the bird removes the clavicles, the sternum, and the ribs, and so on all the way to the anal cavity. The intestines are removed together with the bones. The skin of the neck is left attached to the body, and this is used to close up the incision at the back after the goose has been stuffed, without damaging the breast and taking care not to pull the skin too tight as it would become too fragile later during cooking

To do this successfully it is important to ensure that all the cartilage is removed.

This method can be used when the goose has not been commercially butchered. (European legislation governing butchering stipulates that geese must be sold with the body already eviscerated.)

2. FROM THE ANAL OPENING

This method should be used when the goose was bought already eviscerated and it would be undesirable to make a second cut behind the neck. To bone the bird start from the pelvic cavity and gradually remove the bones starting from the pelvis and working upward, always using a sharp knife and taking care not to damage the skin. The end result is not the same as with the first method.

3. FROM THE BACK

This method should be used when the goose is to be rolled or when an innovative, color-contrasted stuffing is to be used. A cut is first made along the backbone and the carcass is gradually cut away from the meat with a small knife ending with the cartilage of the breast. The goose is then sewn up all along the back.

HOW TO BONE THE THIGH

If the goose is whole, the aim is to cut the skin from below the sternum, and at the back on a level with the kidneys, so as to have as much of it as possible. The legs are usually cut below the joint to avoid damaging the tendons of the thigh so that the thigh itself can be treated like a little bag.

After removing the thigh from the body, a cut is made from the top of the hip down to the knee joint turning the meat back. Without damaging the skin, the bone is removed by cutting it away from the cartilage with a circular movement, thereby leaving the shank itself intact. Thighs that are cut up commercially and sold in this form are also usually cut below the joint a little above the foot.

HOW TO BLANCH THE LIVER

This procedure is normally carried out before all the others. It consists of plunging the liver into boiling water, acidulated with vinegar or a few drops of lemon juice, and leaving it there for a very few minutes (the exact length of time will vary according to the weight of the liver). It is then removed and immediately put into cold water.

Another method is to immerse the liver in cold running water for several hours. This is the method recommended for the liver of older birds, as it removes any disagreeable odor they may have as well as firming the liver up and making it paler in color. It is especially advisable where the liver has been left inside the animal and has not been vacuum-packed. *Foie gras* is not blanched, however, except in the case of certain very particular recipes.

<hr>

COOKING TIMES

BREAST
Goose breast is normally served rare or at least slightly pink, and rapid cooking is therefore preferred. Whole breasts weighing about 9¾ to 10½ oz/280 to 300 g should be cooked for about 15 minutes at 430°F/220°C until browned. Cooking time is increased if stuffing has been added.

THIGH
Goose thigh requires a longer cooking time than breast meat, although in modern cuisine the thigh meat from young birds should also preferably be kept slightly pink. Using traditional cooking methods, thighs from young geese require about 50-60 minutes cooking time while those from older or heavier birds need 70-90 minutes. Using modern technology and fan-assisted ovens these times can be reduced

considerably. More traditional methods are usually used, however, as the thighs are an ingredient in traditional recipes requiring long, slow cooking.

STUFFED THIGH
Stuffed goose thigh is always given fairly long cooking times whether roasted, boiled or braised: it should always be partly stewed in order to prevent it from drying out too much. Thighs should always be cooked gently, even when boiling, to prevent the stitches from coming out. If you have a roasting thermometer, stuffed thigh should be cooked until the temperature at the center reaches 175°F/80°C. Otherwise it should be cooked for at least 1½ hours, whatever cooking method is chosen.

WHOLE ROAST GOOSE
A whole goose for cooking as a roast in the traditional manner weighs around 8¾ to 11 lb/ 4 to 5 kg. Brown it evenly all over, then roast it for about 2 ½ hours at 355-375°F/180-90°C. This cooking time can be reduced with a fan-assisted oven or if the meat is preferred slightly pink.

A young goose weighing 6½ lb/3 kg should be cooked for about 1½ hours, but if cooking it rapidly at a high temperature (430°F/220°C) 50 to 55 minutes will suffice.

STUFFED WHOLE ROAST GOOSE
A stuffed adult goose weighing a generous 13 lb/ 6 kg and filled with a generous 2 lb/1 kg of stuffing should be roasted for at least 2½ hours at 340-355°F/170-180°C to ensure that it is well

cooked and that the stuffing will not crumble when the goose is carved. It should be browned first, and then during cooling the bird should be pricked and basted with the cooking juices.

BOILED GOOSE SALAMI
This is made using the goose neck as a casing, stuffed either with goose meat alone or with a mixture of goose and pork. A salami weighing a generous 2 lb/1 kg should be cooked gently for 1 hour. To prevent it from breaking while cooking, the salami is wrapped in gauze, which is removed before serving.

<hr>

THE RECIPES

GOOSE STOCK

The carcass of a goose weighing 8¾-11 lb/ 4-5 kg
2 carrots
2 onions
2 ribs of celery
3½ oz/100 g of bacon, chopped
1 bouquet garni containing parsley, sage, rosemary
and bay
2 cloves of garlic
25 cups/6 l of water
a pinch of salt

1. Bone the goose carcass and chop into pieces. Put the meat in an ovenproof dish with the

chopped bacon and place in a hot oven at 430-480°F/220-250°C until browned, stirring occasionally.

2. Add the vegetables and return to the oven for a further 15-20 minutes.

3: Remove all the ingredients and transfer them to a large braising pan or saucepan. Add the water, the bouquet garni and a pinch of salt. Bring to a boil, skim off the froth and fat, and simmer for at least 5 hours, skimming off the froth and fat occasionally.

4. Strain the broth through a colander or large strainer.

RISOTTO

3 cups/600 g of short-grain rice
1 onion
2 tbsp of oil
½ glass white wine
8 cups/2 l of skimmed meat stock
4 tsp/20g of butter
3 tbsp/30 g grated cheese

Every region has its own recipe. In my part of the world, risotto is made as follows:

1. Finely chop the onion and fry it gently in a little oil. Add the rice and fry it without allowing the onion to brown too much.

2. Pour in the white wine, allow to evaporate and then add the hot stock. The rice will be cooked in 14-15 minutes. Whisk over a low heat with a little butter and grated cheese.

WHITE POLENTA

¾ cup/350 g finely ground wholemeal
white maize flour
coarse salt
water

1. Pour 6 cups of water into a thick-bottomed saucepan or copper pot. Bring to a boil, salt, and sprinkle in the maize flour, using a whisk to prevent it from forming lumps.

2. Continue to stir over a low heat for about 50 minutes, using a long thick wooden spoon. The polenta should be creamy but not firm. If it solidifies too much, add some more boiling water during cooking.

BRIOCHE

To make a brioche loaf weighing about 14 oz/ 400 g:

7½ tbsp of flour
2 tbsp of butter, melted
2 tsp of brewer's yeast
1 tbsp of sugar
6½ tbsp of milk
the yolk of 2 eggs

1. Mix all the ingredients into a smooth, soft dough. Cover and leave to rise for 50 minutes in a warm, draft-free place.

2. Knead the dough again. Lightly grease a cake tin; put the dough into it, cover and leave to stand again for at least 1½ hours in a warm place.

3. Brush the surface lightly with a mixture of melted butter and water, and bake for 20 minutes at 320°F/160°C.

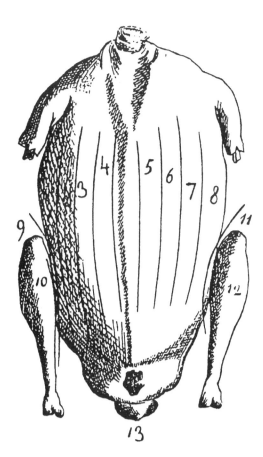

The Recipes of Germano Pontoni

Born in Udine, Germano Pontoni was only 11 years old when he first began to work in the kitchen. He went on to attend catering college, then specialized and began his career as a chef in hotels and aboard cruise ships. He worked as a catering college instructor and, some time later, became head of the catering department of the regional institute for physical medicine and rehabilitation, to which he has brought all his skill and training as a dietician.

Throughout his working life, Pontoni has always devoted a great deal of time and enthusiasm to gastronomical research in the field; his greatest passion is rediscovering the gastronomical traditions of his own region, Friuli. Friuli is home to a deep-rooted, centuries-old tradition of rearing geese, and – almost inevitably – Pontoni has become increasingly interested in these birds.

Goose with salmon trout and asparagus

Serves 6

1 whole goose breast, skinned and weighing a generous 1 lb/500 g, 5 oz/150 g of salmon trout fillets, 4 thin slices of bacon
1 leek, 1 lb 5 oz/600 g of green-tipped asparagus, ½ cup of extra virgin olive oil,
lemon juice, salt, freshly ground white pepper

Method: 1. Clean and wash the leek, cut it into thin rounds and parboil in boiling salted water.

2. Cut the goose breast open and hammer it out thoroughly to obtain a large, wide slice. Salt it lightly. Cut the salmon trout fillet into thin slices and arrange them on top of the goose breast. Sprinkle over the thin rounds of leek.

3. Roll up carefully and wrap in cellophane, fastening it at the sides, and mold into a perfect sausage-shape. Steam for 25 minutes and allow to cool.

4. Steam the asparagus whole, cut off the tips and refresh them in cold water so that they retain their strong green color. Purée the rest of the shoots by pressing through a vegetable mill, dress the purée with oil,

a few drops of lemon juice (optional) and salt, and blend in a food processor to obtain a creamy sauce.

5. Remove the cellophane and slice the goose and salmon trout roll.

6. Pour asparagus sauce over the bottom of each plate, arrange three slices of the roll on top, overlapping them slightly, place a dozen asparagus tips beside them and garnish with a pair of small, shiny lemon leaves.

Wines:

Sauvignon Alto Adige
or a classic Soave

Goose breast larded with cured ham

Serves 6

1 medium-sized goose breast in its skin, weighing 1 lb 5 oz/600 g, 5 oz/150 g prosciutto in a single slice,
9 oz/250 g of corn salad or lamb's lettuce, part of a goose carcass, cut into fairly small pieces, 1 small shallot,
1 clove of garlic, 1 rib of celery, a bouquet garni containing rosemary, thyme and sage, extra virgin olive oil, salt

Method: 1. Cut the goose breast in half.

2. Cut 6 long sticks out of the prosciutto and force them into the two goose breasts to lard the meat. Salt.

3. Place a frying pan on the heat and when it is very hot place the two pieces of goose breast in it, skin side down, and brown them in their own fat.

4. Transfer some of this goose fat to a separate frying pan and use it to quickly brown the vegetables and pieces of the goose carcass.

5. Drain off the fat from the two browned goose breasts and add them to the mixture; cover with a lid and cook over a moderate heat for 20 minutes, basting with a little water only if it becomes too dry.

6. Allow the breast to cool, then cut it into slices. Strain the cooking juices. Dress a few leaves of corn salad with oil and salt and arrange them on a plate. Arrange the slices of goose beside them in a fan shape, and brush with the cooking juices.

Wines:

Pignolo di Buttrio
or Chianti di Gaiole

Terrine of goose with pistachios and muscatel raisins

Serves 10

1 goose, boned and skinned, weighing about 4½ lb/2 kg, 7 oz/200 g of firm bacon, very thinly sliced, ½ glass of brandy, 1 glass of white wine, 10 tbsp of lard, very finely sliced, 4 tbsp of pistachios, shelled and peeled, 4 tbsp of Muscatel raisins, softened in hot water, lemon, roasted pistachios, salt, pepper

Method: 1. Take the goose breasts, cut them in three lengthways and marinade for 5-6 hours in a mixture of the brandy and the white wine.
2. Mince the remainder of the meat, using a coarse setting for one half of it and a fine grinding setting for the other half. Mix the two lots of mince together, and season with a little salt and pepper.
3. Remove the breasts from the marinade, dry them with kitchen paper and wrap them in the bacon.
4. Line a cast-iron terrine with the lard, arrange the minced meat in the bottom using a piping-bag or a bag without a nozzle so as to mold it into shape, and then place a layer of the breast slices wrapped in bacon on top of it together with a few pistachios and Muscatel raisins. Follow with another layer of minced meat, then another layer of breast. Finish with a layer of lard.

5. Cook the terrine in a low oven (355°F/180°C) for 2 hours. Remove from the oven, place a weight (of about 4-5 lb/ 2 kg) on top and allow to cool, first in a cool place and then in the refrigerator for at least 24 hours.

Wines:

*Refosco di Sagrado
or dry Monastir Muscatel*

Salad of summer vegetables and herbs with strips of goose

Serves 6

1 goose breast in its skin, a generous 2 lb/1 kg of cherry tomatoes, 1 red onion,
½ cup of extra virgin olive oil, 1 tbsp of red wine vinegar (preferably mild),
salt, freshly ground pepper, fresh basil leaves for garnish

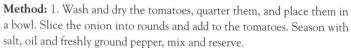

Method: 1. Wash and dry the tomatoes, quarter them, and place them in a bowl. Slice the onion into rounds and add to the tomatoes. Season with salt, oil and freshly ground pepper, mix and reserve.
2. Remove and discard the central bone from the goose breasts, salt the two breasts and brown them in a non-stick frying pan skin side down first, so that they will render their fat. After 10 minutes turn them over and cook until you can tell by pressing on the meat that it is still rare or slightly pink in the middle.
3. Cut the breasts into slices and then into strips.
4. Pour a spoonful of the tomatoes and onions onto individual plates, leaving a hollow in the center, and arrange the strips of goose breast in this. Make a dressing with the olive oil and vinegar; dress the goose meat and garnish with chopped basil leaves.

Wines:

Ciliegiolo di Fonteblanda
or Wildbaker di Pieve di Soligo

Goose salami cooked with pistachios and endive

Serves 8

The neck of a plump goose, to make a salami about 9 in/20 cm long, a generous 10 oz/300 g of goose meat (wing and neck), 3-4 oz/100 g of goose breast, 2 oz/50g bacon, 7 tbsp of shelled green pistachios, black pepper, cayenne pepper, salt, 1 carrot, 1 rib of celery, 1 onion, 1 bay leaf, 2 endives, extra virgin olive oil, balsamic vinegar

Method: 1. Bone the neck of a goose with a very sharp knife, leaving the skin intact. Go over it carefully, removing any veins or cartilage.
2. Mince the meat from the wings and neck, putting it through the mincer twice. Dice the breast and the bacon, mix all these ingredients together well, add salt, black pepper and cayenne pepper, add the pistachios, and mix thoroughly.
3. Sew up one end of the neck using a buttonhole stitch. Stuff the neck and sew up the other end. Do not squeeze the stuffing in too tightly or the neck may tear open during cooking. Prick the neck at several points all over the surface and stick a few toothpicks through it to prevent it bursting during cooking.
4. Peel and chop the vegetables, and put them into cold water. Bring to a boil and boil for 10 minutes, then reduce the heat and carefully add the

neck. Simmer for 40-45 minutes over a low heat.
5. Remove the salami from the stock and wrap it in a dishcloth; place it in the refrigerator with a light weight on top. Remove after a few hours and cut into slices. Dress the endive with the olive oil, salt, and a few drops of balsamic vinegar, and on each plate arrange slices of salami on a bed of endive.

Wines:

*Merlot del Montello
or Marzemino di Isera*

Goose supreme cured in paprika

Serves 6

1 whole goose breast in its skin, 5 oz/150 g of sea salt, 3½ tbsp of sweet paprika, 3½ tbsp of hot paprika,
2 tsp of black peppercorns, 1 tbsp of pepper flavored with clove or allspice,
4 tsp mustard seed or powdered mustard, ½ glass of balsamic vinegar

Method: 1. Cut the goose breast in half and remove all the sinews. Cover a wooden chopping-board with a thin layer of sea salt and place the breast on top. Salt the upper surface of the breast meat too. Tilt the board and leave it like this for at least 24 hours so that the meat loses its liquid. Brush it thoroughly the next day.
2. Grind the mustard. Put the two types of pepper, the paprika, some of the balsamic vinegar and the ground mustard into a small bowl and mix to a thick paste. Completely cover the two breasts with this paste.
3. Attach a thin cord to each one, using a large needle threaded with string, and hang them up to dry in a cool place. Place a plate underneath to catch any liquid. This can be brushed over the breasts from time to time. When they are cured, serve with wholemeal toast lightly spread with butter flavored with radish.

Note: In the Jewish community, the dish is prepared by this method starting 40 days before *Pesach* (Passover).

Wines:

Tazzelenghe
or Barbera d'Alba

Goose liver with Belgian salad au gratin

Serves 4

12 leaves of Belgian endive, 2 ordinary goose livers (not foie gras), 1 shallot, 1 clove of garlic, ½ small glass of brandy,
2 sage leaves, 2 tbsp of breadcrumbs, 1 tbsp of grated parmesan, 1 tbsp of chopped parsley,
salt, pepper, ½ cup of extra virgin olive oil

Method: 1. Blanch the endive leaves in boiling salted water, drain after 2 minutes and plunge into cold water. Drain on kitchen paper.
2. Thoroughly clean and wash the goose livers, and mince them with a knife.
3. Finely mince the shallot and the garlic, and lightly brown them in a frying pan. Add the sage leaves and the minced liver. Season well, adding salt and pepper, and after a few minutes, when the liver starts to take on the consistency of breadcrumbs, pour over the brandy and flambé. (Cook the liver very quickly and only cook it a little, as it will continue to cook when browning in the oven.) Allow to cool. Add a little parmesan and half a tablespoon of breadcrumbs, and shape into long rissoles, which should fill the blanched endive leaves.

4. Mix the remaining breadcrumbs, the cheese, the oil, the parsley and a little salt. Sprinkle this mixture over the rissoles and brown quickly in a very hot oven. Serve hot.

Wines:

Teracrea Malmsey
or Tokay

Maize and smoked goose roll

Serves 6

For the crêpes:
6 tbsp/180 g cornflour, 2 tbsp/60 g flour, 2 eggs, beaten, ⅔ cup/150 ml of milk, ⅔ cup/150 ml of water, 2 tbsp of butter, salt
For the filling:
14 oz/400 g of smoked goose breast, 3½ oz /100 g of hard cheese, 4 cups/1 l of béchamel sauce, not too thick, 2 cups of grated Parmesan,
3½ tbsp of butter, chopped parsley

Method: 1. Pour the milk and water into a mixing bowl. Mix the flour and cornflour together and sprinkle them into the milk and water. Melt the butter and add it to the mixture, then add the salt and the eggs and mix until the mixture has a creamy consistency. It should be just thick enough to coat the back of a spoon. (If it is not thick enough, add more flour).
2. Lightly grease a square or rectangular baking tray (about 13 by 15 in/ 28 by 35 cm). Pour in a ladle of batter or enough batter to cover the bottom of the tray. Place in a very hot oven (480°F/250°C) and remove as soon as the crêpe has browned. Using this method you can make very thin crêpes without turning them. Make 2 crêpes.
3. Slice the goose breast into fine strips. Dice the cheese. Separately, mix 1 cup of the béchamel sauce with the sliced goose breast, the cheese, the grated Parmesan and a little chopped parsley. Mix well, spread a layer of the mixture on a crêpe, cover with another crêpe, spread another layer of filling on the second crêpe and then roll them up to form a roll about 2¾ in/6 cm thick. Refrigerate for 1 hour.
4. Cut the roll into slices about 2½ in/5 cm long and secure with toothpicks. Take six individual heat-resistant dishes and cover with a thin layer of béchamel; arrange two rolls on each, cover with béchamel, Parmesan and melted butter, and brown in hot oven. Remove toothpicks and serve hot.

Wines:

Riesling Renano Alto Adige
or Cabernet Sauvignon dell'Alto Mincio

Miniature gnocchi with shredded goose and pine kernels

Serves 4

7 oz/200 g mixed goose meat (wing, breast scraps, thigh scraps), 1 small shallot, 1 bouquet garni, made up of thyme, parsley and 1 dried bay leaf,
a few fresh basil leaves, 1 glass of dry white wine, 2 tbsp of pine kernels, freshly roasted, ½ cup of extra virgin olive oil
salt, freshly ground black pepper
For the gnocchi:
6½ tbsp of flour, 2 whole eggs, the whites of 2 eggs, a little milk, salt

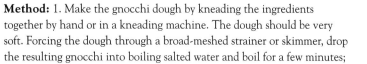

Method: 1. Make the gnocchi dough by kneading the ingredients together by hand or in a kneading machine. The dough should be very soft. Forcing the dough through a broad-meshed strainer or skimmer, drop the resulting gnocchi into boiling salted water and boil for a few minutes; then remove and cool immediately with cold water. This will give small, irregular gnocchi.

2. Shred the goose meat, or cut into fine strips, and place in a bowl; season with a little salt, ground pepper, and the bouquet garni. Leave for at least half a day, so that the meat loses most of its liquid.

3. Lightly brown the shallot in a frying pan with the olive oil, then drain and add the goose meat and brown quickly; pour over the white wine, allow to evaporate and add the pine kernels. Boil the gnocchi again in salted water for a few minutes and sauté all the ingredients together in a large frying pan. If the mixture is too thick, dilute with meat stock.

4. Serve hot, garnished with a few pine kernels and green basil leaves.

Wines:

Lison Tokay
or Biferno Rosso di Campomarino

Semolina and goose shells with herb cheese

Serves 4

1 goose thigh, skin removed, ½ a white onion, 1 rib of celery, 1 carrot, 1 bouquet garni, ¾ cup plus 1 tbsp/200 g of semolina, 1¼ cups of milk, 2 cups of goose stock, 6½ tbsp of butter, 3½ oz/100 g of smoked goose breast, 7 oz/200 g of hard cheese, 2 eggs, beaten, 2 tbsp of grated Parmesan, salt, pepper

Method: 1. Make a stock using the goose thigh, the onion, the celery, the carrot, and the herbs.

2. Bone and finely dice the thigh.

3. Reduce the stock and lightly season with salt. Add the milk and bring to a boil, sprinkle in the semolina and cook for a few minutes. Add the butter. Mix in the eggs and the diced goose and pour out into a wide container so as to allow it to cool slightly.

4. Grease individual heat-resistant dishes. Using a suitable spoon, shape the mixture into a shell shape and arrange portions in each dish; cover each shell shape with thin slices of smoked goose breast, thin slivers of cheese, and a few drops of butter.

5. Brown in a very hot oven and serve hot.

Wines:

*Refosco di Cividale
or Cerasuolo di Vittoria*

Goose margherite* in goose liver and black truffle sauce

Serves 4

For the pasta dough: 3 cups/400 g of flour, 4 eggs, beaten, salt
For the filling: 9 oz/250 g of mixed goose meat, 1 small onion, 1 clove of garlic, 1 tbsp of butter, ½ glass of white wine,
1 stale bread roll, soaked in milk and squeezed out
For the sauce: 1 ordinary goose liver (not foie gras), extra virgin olive oil, 1 cup of stock, salt, freshly ground black pepper,
Parmesan, cut into slivers, black truffle, cut into slivers

Method: 1. Knead the flour and egg into a soft, elastic dough. Cover and set aside to rest.

2. Prepare the filling: chop the onion and cut the meat into small pieces. Chop the onion and brown in the butter with the clove of garlic. Remove the garlic and add the chopped meat. Brown, then pour over the white wine. Season with salt and pepper. Finely mince the meat and mix thoroughly.

3. To make the *marguerite*, finely roll out the pasta dough and cut out circles using a daisy-edged or serrated pastry cutter. Squeeze a little of the filling into the center of each pasta circle using a piping bag without a nozzle, cover with another circle of dough of the same size and seal the edges well, brushing with hot water after squeezing out all the air.

4. Prepare the sauce: dice the liver and brown it quickly in olive oil; pour

over a little stock and season with salt and pepper.

5. Heat water to just below boiling. Plunge in the *margherite* and simmer for about 3 to 4 minutes.

6. Arrange three *margherite* on each of four warmed plates and dress with the sauce. Sprinkle slivers of black truffle and Parmesan on top.

* *Large daisy-shaped ravioli*

Wines:

Cabernet Franc del Collio
or Sagrantino di Montefalco

Tart of miniature gnocchi with smoked goose breast and artichoke hearts

Serves 4

For the pastry:
1½ cups/200 g of flour, 8½ tbsp butter, salt
For the gnocchi:
¾ cup of milk, ⅓ cup of butter, 2½ cups/320g of flour, 3 eggs, beaten, 7 oz / 200 g of Parmesan or other hard cheese, grated,
7 oz/200 g of smoked goose breast, finely shredded, 4 artichoke hearts, 1 clove of garlic, 2 tbsp of extra virgin olive oil, salt, freshly ground pepper

Method: 1. Prepare the pastry: soften the butter and quickly mix in the flour and the salt. Press into a ball and refrigerate for at least 1 hour.
2. Roll out the pastry and cut out 4 circles. Arrange these over 4 upturned bowls or dishes about 1 in/2 cm deep (grease the surface that is in contact with the pastry) and bake in a hot oven. Use these pastry cases as containers in which to bake the gnocchi.
3. Prepare the gnocchi: bring the milk to a boil, add the butter and then sprinkle in the flour to make a paste. Allow to cool, then add the eggs and half the cheese. Using a spoon or a piping bag, drop the gnocchi into boiling water. Drain as soon as they float back to the surface, and cool them immediately in cold water.
4. Cut the artichoke hearts into segments and cook separately in a frying pan with the garlic and oil.

5. Arrange half the artichoke in the pastry cases, then place a layer of gnocchi on top, followed by the remaining artichoke, a generous helping of goose meat, and finally the grated cheese and a few drops of melted butter.
6. Brown in a hot oven and serve immediately.

Wines:

Umbrian Pinot Noir
or Santa Maddalena

Alpine-style smoked goose and vegetable soup

Serves 4

3½ oz/100 g lean goose meat (breast or thigh), 3½ oz/100 g smoked goose breast, thickly sliced, 1 carrot, 1 onion, 1 zucchini, 1 rib of celery, 2 medium-sized potatoes, 1 slice of cabbage (3½ oz /100 g), 8 cups/2 l stock (possibly goose stock), unsalted, salt, freshly ground pepper, 4 slices of rye bread, extra virgin olive oil

Method: 1. Cut the lean goose meat into thin strips. 2. Dice all the vegetables and cook them in a small amount of water, starting with the carrot, potato and celery, and adding the onion and zucchini so that they all finish cooking at the same time without disintegrating. Very lightly season with salt.
3. Quickly sauté the strips of lean goose meat in a little oil and add to the vegetables. Bring the stock to a boil, add it to the meat and vegetables and simmer for a few minutes. Then add the smoked goose meat. The mixture should now have the consistency of a thick soup.

5. Dice the rye bread into croutons and toast them lightly. Pour the soup into a tureen or individual bowls and just before serving, sprinkle on some freshly ground pepper and drizzle over a little extra virgin olive oil. Serve the croutons separately.

Wines:

*Schioppettino di Ipplis or
Lacrima di Morro d'Alba*

Half-moons of potato with ragout of goose and radicchio

Serves 4

10½ oz/300 g of potatoes, boiled, cooled and sieved, 5 tbsp of flour, 1 egg, beaten, 1 tbsp of grappa, salt, 1 pinch of freshly grated nutmeg, 2 goose thighs, with skin, 1 goose carcass, 2 ribs of celery, 2 carrots, 1 white onion, 1 bouquet garni, 2 radicchio, salt, freshly ground pepper

Method: 1. Make a stock using the goose carcass, the skin from the goose thighs, half the vegetables and the bouquet garni.

2. Make a ragout: finely chop half the onion, 1 carrot and 1 rib of celery and mince the meat from the goose thigh; brown the chopped vegetables in a little oil with the minced thigh meat, and when well browned pour over a little stock. Add salt and pepper to taste and continue to cook for about 2½ hours over a very low heat until the mixture forms a thick ragout.

3. Mix the potato with the egg and flour. Roll out the mixture to a thickness of about ⅛ in/3mm and with a pastry cutter cut out circles about 2¼ in/6 cm across. Spoon some of the ragout onto each circle and fold over so as to make half-moons, sealing the edges well.

4. Clean the radicchio and set aside the small leaves from the center to use as a garnish. Slice the remaining leaves, not too finely, and blanch them quickly in boiling water.

5. Strain the goose stock. If it is too thin, reduce it over a low heat until it thickens to a glaze. Cook the half-moons in boiling salted water, and dress them with the glaze.

6. Arrange the half-moons on a plate on a bed of hot parboiled radicchio; drizzle over a few more drops of glaze, garnish with the small leaves from the heart of the radicchio and serve hot.

Wines:

Merlot dei colli Euganei
or Dolcetto d'Alba

Biechi with goose sausages and celery

Serves 4

14 oz/400 g of fresh egg lasagne, 14 oz/400 g of lean goose sausages, 1 glass of white wine, 7 oz/200 g celery, blanched,
3 tbsp extra virgin olive oil, 5 tbsp grated hard mature cheese,
1 ladle of stock, salt

Method: 1. Break the lasagne into roughly diamond-shaped pieces (*biechi*) and cook in boiling salted walter. Drain and reserve.
2. Finely chop a little of the goose sausage and brown in a frying pan without oil. Finely chop and add the celery; brown together, then pour over a little white wine and finally the stock.
3. Remove half of the mixture and blend it in a food processor, with the olive oil. Return it to the frying pan with the rest of the sauce.
4. Prick the remaining sausages and place them in a frying pan with the rest of the wine, cover and cook for 15-20 minutes over a low heat.
5. Stir the *biechi* into the sauce, and pour the mixture onto heated plates; slice the sausages diagonally and arrange one sausage on top of the *biechi* on each plate. Brush the sausages with the juices they were cooked in.

This is quite a highly seasoned, full-flavored dish that does not need further seasoning.

Wines:

Cabernet di Breganze
or Fojaneghe rosso

Potato gnocchi stuffed with goose liver, with field mushrooms and bacon

Serves 6

For the gnocchi: 1½ lb/700 g of potato gnocchi dough (see the recipe for potato half-moons on page 74), 2 ordinary goose livers (not foie gras),
4 or 5 ripe tomatoes, peeled, seeded and diced, ½ glass of dry white wine, 1 bouquet garni, containing sage and a bayleaf, 3½ tbsp of butter, salt, pepper
For the sauce: 21 oz/600 g field mushrooms, 5¼ oz/150 g bacon (in a single piece, not in rashers), 1 small white onion, 1 tbsp tomato concentrate,
chopped parsley, ½ glass of dry white wine, ¼ cup of extra virgin olive oil, ½ a ladle of stock, salt, pepper
For the garnish: 18 slices of cured goose meat, 12 slices of green zucchini, cut lengthwise and grilled

Method: 1. Clean and blanch the livers, then drain and dice them. Finely chop the onion, lightly brown in butter. Add the liver and brown very quickly. Pour over the wine, allow to evaporate, then add the bouquet garni and tomatoes. Simmer for a few minutes and allow to cool.
2. Shape the gnocchi dough into rolls of about 1 in/2 cm across. Flatten each one in the palm of the hand, put a teaspoonful of filling into the hollow, and close the dough so as to form a ball.
3. Prepare the sauce. Finely slice the mushrooms and fry lightly in a very hot pan to make them wilt. Dry them, season with a clove of garlic and oil, and fry over a hot flame. Add the wine and allow to evaporate. Dilute the tomato concentrate in the stock and add to the mixture, continuing to cook over a lower heat until the mushrooms are tender.
4. Cut the bacon into thin strips, brown it, remove the fat and add it to the mushrooms. Add a little stock to dilute the sauce if necessary.
5. Cook the slices of cured goose meat very briefly over a very high heat so that they are just seared. Arrange the slices of zucchini and goose meat in alternating strips around each plate. Cook the gnocchi in boiling salted water, drain them when they float to the surface and arrange (5 per person) on the goose and zucchini. Pour over the sauce and serve hot.

Wines:

Merlot Trentino
or Franconia del Friuli

Roulades of Savoy cabbage with minced goose and rice

Serves 4

8 Savoy cabbage leaves, 12¼ oz/350 g goose meat from wings, neck and trimmings, 1 tbsp of grated Parmesan, 1 leek, ¼ cup/60 g of rice, 1 small shallot, 1¼ cups/300 ml of stock, 2 tbsp of butter, 1 slice of stale bread soaked in milk, 1 egg, ½ glass of dry white wine, 8 thin slices of bacon fat, salt, pepper

Method: 1. Mince the goose meat and mix in the Parmesan, the bread softened in milk, the egg, salt and pepper. Put the mixture through the mincer for a second time, mixing thoroughly, and shape into 8 rissoles.

2. Cut the leek into thin strips and parboil with the cabbage. Place a slice of bacon fat on each cabbage leaf. Roll out the rissoles a little, and put a rissole on top of each leaf. Roll up the cabbage leaves, folding the edges in towards the middle, and tie them so as to make roulades.

3. Finely chop the shallot and brown in a high-sided frying pan. Add the roulades, pour over a little water, simmer for ½ hour. Add more water if necessary.

4. Skim the fat from the surface of the liquid around the roulades and use it to brown the remaining shallot; add the rice, mix thoroughly, turn up the heat and pour over the wine. Cook the rice as for a regular risotto with Parmesan and stock (*see* page 53). Finally, stir in the remaining butter.

5. Serve very hot on individual plates, arranging the roulades (2 per person) on a bed of rice; cut each roulade in two diagonally, and dress with the juices that the roulades were cooked in.

Wines:

Refosco dal Peduncolo Rosso or Inferno Valtellina

Goose salami with diced turnip and celery

Serves 6

*The whole skin of a goose neck, a generous pound/500 g of goose meat (neck, wing, trimmings of breast), 3½ oz /100 g of pork fat, 1 goose liver,
1 slice of stale bread, the crust removed, soaked in milk, 1 carrot, 1 rib of celery, salt, allspice or Jamaica pepper
For the side dish: 1 lb 5 oz/600 g of young turnip, 1 lb 5 oz/600 g of celeriac, 1 tbsp vinegar or the juice of ½ a lemon, extra virgin olive oil,
balsamic or herb-flavored vinegar, salt, freshly ground black pepper*

Method: 1. Finely mince the scraps of goose meat. Squeeze out and add the bread, salt and pepper, and put the mixture through the mincer again.
2. Chop the goose meat and the pork fat into small pieces, and blanch and dice the liver. Add these ingredients to the mixture. Sew up one end of the goose neck using a buttonhole stitch. Stuff the neck, without squeezing the stuffing in too tightly, and sew up the other end. Wrap the neck in a piece of gauze or a loose-weave dishcloth and immerse it in hot water with the carrot and celery.
3. Simmer for about 1 hour. (To prevent the neck from bursting, stick a few toothpicks through it). When it is cooked, remove from the stock and keep hot. (The strained stock is delicious on its own or can be used to make a minestrone-type soup.)
4. Peel the turnips (if their skin is tender they need only be washed). Dice them into cubes a finger thick. Peel and dice the celeriac. Boil separately in acidulated salted water. Drain and mix them together while still hot. Just before serving dress with the oil, balsamic or herb vinegar, salt and pepper.
5. Slice the goose salami, allowing at least three slices per portion, and serve with a large spoonful of vegetables on each plate.

Wines:

*Barbera di Rochetta Tanaro or
Blaufrankisch di Cormons*

Goose stew with white polenta

Serves 8

1 small to medium-sized goose, 3 small white onions, 2 leeks, 3 cloves, 2 glasses of dry white wine,
a handful of capers, 4 anchovy fillets, 1 whole end prosciutto weighing 7 oz/200 g, 2 cloves of garlic, 3 bay leaves, salt and pepper, white polenta

Method: 1. Clean the goose, setting aside the liver and the fat. Joint the goose, allowing 2 or 3 pieces per portion.
2. Thinly slice the onions and put them in a large frying pan or heat-resistant earthenware dish together with the chopped prosciutto, the garlic, the bay leaves and the goose fat. Chop the leek. Cover the pan and simmer. Season the pieces of goose and add to the pan with the cloves, the chopped leek and the liver. Brown all together, then pour over the white wine. Allow to reduce, then cover and continue to cook, adding a little water from time to time.
3. When the meat and vegetables are cooked, remove them from the pan and keep them warm. Add some capers and the anchovy fillets to the stock and whisk it up to make a sauce. Check the seasoning and continue to simmer for a few minutes, then serve accompanied with freshly cooked white polenta (*see* page 53). This dish can be accompanied by a side dish of mixed seasonal salad, with boiled beans and slivers of raw onion.

Wines:

Merlot del Montello
or Bonarda di Godiasco

Stuffed goose with risotto

Serves 8-10

1 medium-sized goose, weighing 5½ lb/2.5 kg when cleaned, 10½ oz/300 g of sausage, skinned, 10½ oz/300 g of veal and lean pork in equal proportions, minced, 1 leek, 2 cloves of garlic, 1 onion, 1 sprig of rosemary, 3 cups/600 g of rice, 3½ tbsp of butter, 1 sachet of saffron, Parmesan, cinnamon, salt and pepper, about 4 cups/1 l of light stock

Method: 1. Cook 7 oz/200 g of the rice, whisking in butter and Parmesan at the end of cooking. Allow to cool.

2. Thoroughly bone the goose, starting from the lower part, without tearing the skin. Salt and pepper the boned goose and leave to stand for at least 1 hour.

3. Prepare the stuffing: mix the veal and pork with the rice and the sausage so as to form an even mixture. Stuff the goose and sew up the ends. (The amount of stuffing used will vary according to the size of the goose: the stuffing must not be squeezed in too tightly, otherwise the skin will burst during cooking).

4. Truss the goose and roast it, basting it with stock and with white wine if desired, and seasoning it with garlic and rosemary. (To make more stock, the bones and scraps that are left over after boning the bird may be added.)

5. When the goose is cooked, wrap it in foil or put it in a container, and keep it warm. Strain the cooking juices.

6. Make a risotto, using the light stock brought to a boil; towards the end of cooking add the saffron. Serve the meat cut into slices and glazed with the cooking juices and accompanied by the risotto.

Wines:

*Sizzano
or Inferno Valtellina*

Goose turnover with barley and vegetable ragout

Serves 8

2 whole goose thighs, the two weighing about 2 lb 10 oz/1.2 kg, 1 onion, 1 rib of celery, 1 carrot, 1 bouquet garni consisting of rosemary, sage and sprigs of parsley, 1½ feet / ½ metre of pork caul, ½ glass of dry white wine, 1¼ cups/300 g of pearl barley, a generous 4 cups/1 l of light stock

Method: 1. Bone the goose thighs and remove the skin. Season the inside of the thighs with salt and pepper. Place the pork caul on a work surface, fold double, and season with salt. Place the thighs one beside the other on the pork caul and roll them up in it. Truss with twine.

2. Place the roll in a high-sided pan, add the wine and place in a medium oven. When the wine has evaporated and the melted fat from the caul can be glimpsed at the bottom of the pan, add the bouquet garni.

3. Cover the pan and return to the oven for another hour, basting from time to time with a little stock. Dice the vegetables and add them to the cooking juices. When the vegetables are cooked (they will need about 20 minutes) the roll will also be ready (only a few drops of clear or pale liquid should trickle out when it is pricked with a fork). Remove from the pan and set aside. Drain the vegetables and strain the cooking juices; these should be thick enough to be used as a sauce (if necessary reduce them).

4. Cook the barley with the Parmesan in the same way as risotto, adding boiling light stock from time to time. After ¾ hour add the vegetables that were cooked with the meat. When the barley is cooked, leave to stand.

5. Cut the roll into slices. The cooking juices should be thick enough to be used as a sauce. On each plate arrange a spoonful of barley and two slices of goose turnover. Dress with the cooking juices. Serve hot.

Wines:

Isonzo Rosso or
Squinzano Riserva

Fried goose medallions with apples and sage

Serves 4

14 oz/400 g of goose meat scraps (such as trimmings from breast, wings and thighs), 1 stale bread roll softened in milk, 8 leaves of fresh sage, 2 cups of oil for frying, 2 eggs, beaten, 4 tbsp of flour, 8 tbsp of white breadcrumbs, salt, pepper, 1 pinch of ground cumin seed, 2 unripe apples such as Golden Delicious

Method: 1. Remove any skin from the meat and put it through a mincer twice, crumbling up and adding the softened bread.
2. Shape the mixture into 12 small rissoles (3 per serving) and press into medallions. Peel the apples, remove the core and slice them into rounds about ¼ in/½ cm thick.
3. Clean the sage leaves with a sheet of kitchen paper. Dip the sage, the apple and the goose medallions in the flour, then in the egg and finally coat them with the breadcrumbs. Fry them in hot oil, starting with the sage, following with the apple and finishing with the goose medallions.
4. Serve all together, very hot, on dishes lined with paper doilies or absorbent serviettes, and sprinkled with salt and cumin seed.

Wines:

*Grignolino d'Asti
or Barbera dei Colli Bolognesi*

Goose breast
with mandarins and cinnamon

Serves 4

*1 whole goose breast, or separate pieces, weighing about 1 lb 5 oz/600g, 3 large mandarins, 1 glass sparkling or dry white wine,
1 small spice sachet containing cinnamon sticks and 1 bay leaf, 1 ladle of stock, ½ tbsp of butter, 1 tbsp of extra virgin olive oil, ½ tsp of sugar, salt,
freshly ground green, pepper, 1 tsp cornflour*

Method: 1. Divide the goose breast into two, removing the central cartilage and any fatty deposits but leaving the skin on. Season thoroughly with green pepper and salt, and leave the meat to absorb these flavors for about ½ hour.

2. Brown the breasts skin side down first in a pan with a little oil, then turn them over and cook for another 15 minutes until lightly browned. Pour over the dry white wine and drain immediately; remove the breasts from the cooking juices.

3. Add the sachet of spices, the juice of 1 mandarin and a little stock. Allow to boil for 10 minutes, thicken with the cornflour and strain.

4. Dissolve the sugar in a very small amount of hot water and brush over the skin of the breasts, then grill them. Brush them a second time and return to the grill. Repeat until the skins are a reddish golden color.

5. Using a very sharp knife, peel the segments of 2 mandarins. Add the butter to the sauce and whip, beating thoroughly.

6. Thinly slice the goose breasts and arrange them, slightly overlapping, in a serving dish. Garnish with the mandarin segments, and pour over the sauce made from the cooking juices. Serve very hot. The meat should be slightly pink in the middle.

Wines:

*Romagno Rosso
or Rubesco Riserva*

Boiled goose thighs with turnip stuffing

Serves 6

3 plump goose thighs, 2 onions, 2 ribs of celery, 2 carrots, chopped parsley, 3½ oz /100 g boiled turnip, 1¾ oz / 50 g mature hard cheese, 1½ cups/100 g breadcrumbs, 2 eggs, beaten, salt, pepper, extra virgin olive oil (for dressing), wine vinegar (for dressing)

Method: 1. Bone the thighs (*see* page 51) without damaging the meat.
2. Dice the turnip and grate the cheese. Prepare the stuffing, mixing together the bread, the grated cheese, the eggs, salt and pepper and the diced turnip.
3. Stuff the thighs (not too tightly) and sew up both ends with white thread (when the thighs are cooked, this will be removed together with the first slice at the moment of serving). Wrap the thighs in a kitchen towel and fasten securely.

4. Boil the thighs in water for about 2 hours, with the onion, the celery and the carrot, adding salt to taste. Remove the thighs from the towel and allow to cool.
5. Dice the vegetables used to make the cooking stock. Slice the thighs and arrange them on a bed of diced vegetables, dressed with a mixture of oil, a little vinegar and salt.

Wines:

*Garda Bresciano Rosso
or Dolcetto di Dogliani*

Stuffed goose thighs with steamed Savoy cabbage

Serves 6

3 goose thighs, 3 pork sausages, skin removed, 6 large leaves of Savoy cabbage, blanched, a few leaves of sage, 1 glass of dry white wine, 1 tbsp of flour, salt, pepper, a little vegetable stock, ½ cup of vinegar, 1 tbsp extra virgin olive oil

Method: 1. Bone the goose thighs, remove all the veins and sinews, and flatten them out. Lay a cabbage leaf and a sausage on each one; roll them up and fasten with buttonhole stitch. Season with salt and pepper and coat with flour.

2. Prick the thighs with a needle and lay them in a non-stick frying pan. With no additional fat, cover and cook over a low heat so that they lose their fat. When they are evenly browned all over, remove the fat and pour the white wine over the thighs; allow to evaporate and add the sage.

3. Cook gently for 1 hour, if necessary adding a little more stock to supplement the cooking juices. When they are cooked, remove the thighs and set aside, covered and weighed down so as to squeeze out more of the fat.

3. Dilute the cooking juices to the desired consistency and season with salt and pepper. Parboil the remaining cabbage leaves in salted water with some vinegar added. Drain and cut into shreds.

4. Slice the thighs and arrange on a hot serving dish. Garnish with the cabbage dressed with a little olive oil and seasoned with pepper.

Wines:

Bramaterra
or Rosso di Cercatoia

Goose breast with muscatel grapes and apple vinegar

Serves 6

1 whole lean goose breast weighing about 1 lb 7 oz/650 g, 1 tbsp of red wine vinegar, ½ glass Merlot or other sweet wine, freshly ground black pepper, coarse salt, 1 pinch of sweet marjoram, 3 tbsp of flour, ½ cup of extra virgin olive oil, 1 tbsp of butter, 3 tbsp of apple vinegar, 1 small ladle of stock, about 40 large muscatel grapes

Method: 1. Skin the goose breast and divide it into its two halves. Using a sharp knife, cut the breast in six escalopes. Flatten them slightly with a meat pounder, laying a cloth on them so as to prevent them from breaking up. Rub them lightly with the salt and pepper, then place them in a dish and sprinkle with the wine vinegar and the wine, and add the marjoram. Marinate for at least 1 hour, stirring and turning from time to time.

2. Dry the escalopes with kitchen paper, coat them with flour and gently brown them in a pan with oil and butter, removing them just before they are completely cooked. Cover with foil and keep warm.

3. Add the apple vinegar to the cooking juices in the pan, and mix well to scrape away and blend in any residues stuck to the pan. Add the stock and reduce until the cooking juices are slightly thickened and strain. (If the liquid is too thin, sprinkle in ½ tsp cornflour and cook for a few moments longer.) Peel and pit the grapes; add them to the cooking juices and let them absorb the flavors. Add salt to taste.

4. Take six plates and pour some of the sauce onto each one. Place one escalope on the sauce with at least six grapes and a little more sauce, and garnish with a few marjoram leaves. Serve hot.

Wines:

*Salice Salentino Rosso
or Teroldego*

Goose and pear slices with Merlot

Serves 4

*1 whole goose breast weighing about 1 lb 5 oz/600 g, 2 William pears, or similar variety, fairly ripe, 1 glass of Merlot wine,
1 tsp cornstarch, 1 small handful of shelled green pistachios, flaked or crushed, 1 tbsp of butter, salt, freshly ground pepper,
4 cloves, the grated zest of ½ a lemon*

Method: 1. Divide the goose breasts into two, keeping the skin on but removing the cartilage. Season with salt and pepper and leave the breasts to stand for at least ½ hour.

2. Peel the pears and remove the core. Cut them in half and press a clove into each piece. Steam for about 5 minutes with the lemon zest, then cool immediately.

3. Brown the two goose breasts in a frying pan with a little butter, then reduce the heat and cook for about 15 minutes more (they should be soft to the touch). Remove from the pan, wrap in foil and keep warm. Pour the wine into the pan and scrape away and blend in any residue. Thicken the liquid with cornstarch and then warm in a double boiler.

5. Just before serving, slice the pears and the goose meat. Arrange the slices on each plate overlapping in a fan shape, and alternating a slice of pear with a slice of goose. Add the butter to the sauce and whisk vigorously until it has a bright, glossy sheen. Glaze each serving and garnish with pistachios. Serve hot.

Wines:

*Merlot di Borghetto d'Avio
or Colle Picchioni Rosso*

Goose breast
with pineapple and almonds

Serves 4

6 fillets of goose (the cut taken from behind the breast proper), 3-4 tbsp of flour, 1 small pineapple, complete with its crown of leaves,
1 cup of unsweetened pineapple juice, 1 small glass of brandy, 1 tbsp of white wine vinegar, salt, freshly ground white pepper,
1 tbsp butter, 1 tbsp blanched almonds

Method: 1. Coat fillets of goose in flour and brown them in a little butter until just underdone. Salt them and pour over the brandy. Remove the fillets from the pan, wrap in film and foil.
2. To the juices in the pan add the pineapple juice and the vinegar, heat to thicken and strain. Peel the pineapple, reserving the top with the leaves, and cut the flesh into small segments. Return the juices to the pan, add the fresh pineapple segments and allow the liquid to reduce until it forms a thick sauce. Remove the pineapple segments and add the remaining butter.
3. Cut the goose fillets diagonally so as to form long, oblique slices. Place the top of the pineapple with the leaves in the center of an oval dish and arrange the goose fillets and pineapple segments around it. Thicken the

sauce with the butter and pour a little over the dish. Chop the almonds, lightly toast them in the oven and sprinkle them on the dish.
4. Serve the rest of the sauce separately. (If there is not enough sauce or if it is too thick, add a little stock. The flavor may also be sharpened with the addition of a few drops of lemon juice.)

Wines:

Carignano del Sulcis
or Traminer del Collio

Three rules concerning foie gras

Those who appreciate *foie gras* know that three golden rules apply to the creation of an excellent and aristocratic *foie gras* dish.

The first rule concerns the choice. A good liver should weigh between 1 lb 7 oz/650 g and 1 lb 10 oz/750 g when raw, and should come from a full-grown goose weighing between 9 lb/ 4 kg and 10 lb/ 4.5 kg that has been fattened on cooked white maize. If the bird is heavier than this, the liver becomes too fat and tends to disintegrate during cooking, losing the consistency and texture that ensures its exquisite taste.

The second rule is not to over-season or flavor the dish, and thus risk masking the unique taste of the

foie gras, particularly when following simpler, more traditional recipes. This also applies to the preparation of *foie gras* for preserving in terrines or other containers for long periods. If the *foie gras* is too strongly seasoned its classic flavor will be lost, while if it is not properly covered in goose fat it will be exposed to the air and will not keep.

The third rule is that *foie gras* must be cooked over a low heat and with great care.

For the real lover of *foie gras*, nothing goes better with this delicacy than a slice of home-made bread, a glass of fine wine and the time to savor it in all its simplicity.

Terrine of foie gras with brioche

Serves 6

1 good-quality goose liver weighing between 1 lb 7 oz/650 g and 1 lb 9 oz/700 g, 2 cups milk, 1 tsp sugar, 1 fresh bay leaf,
salt, black or green pepper, freshly ground, 1 glass of good-quality brandy, 2 cups of Marsala, not too dry,
a few slices of very fine white bacon fat

Method: 1. Pour half the milk into a dish large enough to hold the whole liver. Divide the liver into its two lobes, remove the veins and add it to the milk. Add the sugar and the bay leaf. Cover with the remaining milk and leave to macerate for at least 24 hours in a cool place.
2. Remove the liver, drain it and cut both pieces in half again lengthwise. Working with cool hands, taper the pieces of liver to the length of the dish in which it is to be cooked. Salt the liver and pepper it with either black or green pepper.
3. Immerse the liver in a mixture of brandy and Marsala and leave to macerate for another day.
4. Line an ovenproof terrine with the bacon fat, arrange the liver in it and cover with another layer of bacon fat. Put the terrine in a double boiler in the oven and cook at a temperature not exceeding 165°F/75°C for about 15 minutes or 20 minutes at most (the liver should still be pale pink in the middle). Cool in the refrigerator, in the same terrine.
5. Serve in the terrine, accompanied with hot slices of brioche lightly toasted on both sides.

Wines:

Gewürztraminer Alto Adige
or Planargia Malmsey

Simple foie gras

1 goose foie gras
finely ground sea salt
freshly ground black pepper

Method: 1. Carefully remove the large vein and the green traces of bile from the *foie gras*. Handle the liver as little as possible, keeping it cold until the moment of cooking.

2. Place the *foie gras* on a work surface and season with salt and pepper. (If the *foie gras* is of the right size, it should not be excessively salted.)

3. Place the *foie gras* in a frying pan (preferably non-stick), without adding any fat and without covering it. Cook over a low heat, taking care to move it by gently shaking the pan. Turn it with a wooden spatula without damaging the membrane. After 25 minutes the *foie gras* will be done, and will have lost its excess fat.

4. Place the *foie gras* in a terrine or a casserole dish with a lid. Cover it in its own fat and place in the refrigerator.

5. The *foie gras* can be eaten two or three days later, but it is even better if left for a week. Serve with toasted farmhouse-style bread such as ciabatta. A few Muscat grapes also make a delicious accompaniment to this dish.

Wines:

Alto Adige Rosé Muscatel
or Bosa Malmsey

Escalopes of foie gras with a Picolit glaze

Serves 6

1 goose foie gras weighing between 1 lb 7 oz/650 g and 1 lb 9 oz/700 g, ⅔ cup/150 ml of Picolit, 1 zucchini, 1 small carrot, 2 ribs of white celery, 1 tbsp of white apple vinegar, 2 tbsp of extra virgin olive oil, 1 bay leaf, salt and pepper to taste, 2 tbsps flour, green salad leaves such as lambs lettuce

Method: 1. Thoroughly clean the *foie gras* and remove veins if necessary. Cut it into thin slices (3 or 4 per person), cutting across the breadth. Arrange the slices on a large dish, cover them with Picolit, and leave to macerate for at least 4 hours.

2. Cut the zucchini, the carrot and the celery into julienne strips and blanch them in boiling salted water. Drain and set aside.

3. Dry the *foie gras* escalopes with absorbent paper, coat them with flour and brown them quickly in a non-stick frying pan, seasoning with the bay leaf. Salt very lightly.

4. Just before serving, arrange some of the julienne of vegetables in the bottom of each individual plate, with a few salad leaves; dress with a vinaigrette made with the extra virgin olive oil and the vinegar. Lay the escalopes of liver on the bed of vegetables. Deglaze the frying pan with the Picolit used for the marinade, strain the cooking juices over the escalopes and serve. The sauce should be slightly thick.

Wine:

Picolit

Focaccia with goose crackling

Serves 6

1¼ cups/150 g of flour, a generous pound/500 g of fine goose skin, 2 tbsp/30 g butter, 2 tbsp olive oil, 1 tbsp yeast,
½ cup of milk, 1 tsp of salt

Method: 1. Knead a handful of flour together with half the yeast dissolved in a little milk, to form a soft dough. Shape it into a small loaf, put it in a warm place and leave it to rise for at least ½ hour.
2. Clean the goose skin, cut it into fine strips, and heat them slowly in a non-stick frying pan so that they lose their fat. Then squeeze them out so as to remove all the fat. Remove them from the frying pan and cool.
3. Make a heap of the remaining flour, crumble the rest of the yeast into it, add the softened butter, the oil, the salt, the crackling and the risen ball of dough, and knead well together. If the dough is too stiff, add a little milk. Continue kneading until the dough forms small bubbles.
4. Roll out the dough to a thickness of ¼ in/ ½ cm.

5. Grease and flour a round or rectangular baking tin, arrange the dough in it and make criss-cross cuts on the surface. Bake in a pre-heated oven at 390°F/200°C for about 1 hour without opening the oven.

Note: This loaf makes a delicious country-style snack, especially if stuffed with goose charcuterie or goose salami.

Wines:

Lambrusco Salamino
or Barbera Vivace Oltrepò

Biscuits with Tokay and goose fat

Make 2 generous pounds/1 kg of biscuits

4 cups/500 g of flour, ⅔ cup/150 ml of white Tokay,
⅓ cup/80 g of light extra virgin olive, ⅓ cup/80 g of goose fat,
½ cup plus 2 tbsp/150 g of sugar

1. Make a heap of the flour and pour the wine, the softened goose fat, the sugar and the oil into the middle. Knead slowly but very thoroughly until it forms a soft dough.
2. Roll out to a thickness of about ⅛ in/3 mm and cut out as many round biscuits, about 2½ in/5 cm in diameter, as possible. Make a small hole in the middle of each one with a serrated pastry cutter.

3. Grease a baking tray, arrange the biscuits on it and bake in a pre-heated oven at 355°F/180°C for about 20 minutes.

Note: This unusual biscuit originated in the Jewish community but has undergone various changes over the years. The light goose fat, once so widely used, makes this country-style biscuit particularly crumbly.

Wines:

Strevi Muscatel
or Fragolino Bianco

Fried custard creams in zabaglione sauce

Serves 4

⅓ cup/80 g of caster sugar, 2½ tbsp of flour, the zest of half a lemon, 2 goose eggs, 2 cups/500 ml of milk, boiled and cooled,
a little rose water, salt, 1 vanilla bean, sticks of cinnamon, breadcrumbs, butter for frying
For the zabaglione: the yolk of 1 goose egg, 10 tbsp/150 g of sugar, 2 cups/500 ml of Schioppettino wine

Method: 1. Beat one whole egg and one yolk in a bowl together with 4 tbsp of milk, the sugar, and the flour. Set aside. Pour the remaining milk into a saucepan with the lemon zest and a pinch of salt. Bring to a boil, then drizzle into the egg, flour and sugar mixture, mixing constantly. Pour the liquid into a saucepan, add a vanilla bean and bring to a boil, stirring constantly. Simmer for 5 minutes, then remove from the heat and flavor with 1 tbsp of rose water. Remove the lemon zest and the vanilla.
2. Spread custard cream out in a wide dish to a thickness of 1 in/2 cm and leave to cool. Lightly beat an egg white with a fork. Then cut the custard cream into diamond shapes and coat these first with the lightly beaten egg white, then with breadcrumbs. Make sure that each diamond is completely covered with both ingredients.

3. Prepare the zabaglione. Beat the egg yolk together with the sugar until the mixture turns pale. Add the wine and cook in a double boiler, stirring with a whisk. The zabaglione should be creamy and pink.
4. Fry the custard creams in plenty of butter until they are golden brown and crisp on the outside. Lay them out on a plate covered in kitchen paper to absorb the excess fat, then arrange them on a serving dish and serve immediately, with the zabaglione sauce.

Wines:

Fragolino Rosso or
Castelnuovo Don Bosco Malmsey

The goose in the modern Italian repertoire

Having languished in almost total oblivion for many years, goose meat and goose liver have made a strong comeback in the world of haute cuisine thanks to a renewed interest in rediscovering our gastronomic heritage. Here, then, is an impressive collection of recipes from chefs working in every part of Italy. They present the goose in a range of dishes, some of refined simplicity, others of great sophistication, but all of the greatest gastronomic excellence.

STARTERS

Spring goose

Serves 6-8

1 goose, weighing about 4½ lb/2 kg to 6½ lb/3 kg, 1 cup of extra virgin olive oil, ½ cup of water, salt, pepper, rosemary, garlic, bay leaf

This goose-meat preserve is best made in the late fall to early winter, to be eaten in the spring.
Method: 1. Clean the goose and cut it into pieces, removing the dorsal bones, the feet, and the tips of the wings.
2. Place the goose in a cooking pot together with all the other ingredients, cover with a lid and roast at 300°F/150°C for about 3 hours. During cooking, the fat should not fry but simmer.

3. Drain the pieces of goose and arrange them, still hot, in preserving jars together with the herbs they were cooked in and cover with the strained fat. Seal the jars, making sure that they are airtight. Store in a dark place, such as a cellar, and do not touch for at least 2 months.
5. Remove the pieces of meat, fillet them cold and garnish with fresh salad and nuts. Dress with extra virgin olive oil and balsamic vinegar.

Wines:

*Verduzzo di San Giovanni al Natisone
or rosé Alezio*

Goose terrine

Serves 25

2 lb/900 g of goose breast, 1 lb 5 oz/600 g of pork fat, diced, 7 oz/200 g of goose fat, diced,
9 oz/250 g of pork fillet, cut into 3 pieces, 3½ tbsp of lard, 1 bouquet garni, containing sage, parsley, whole white peppercorns, bay leaf, and 2 cloves of garlic,
1 carrot, 1 onion, 1 clove of garlic, unpeeled, 2 tsp of freshly ground green pepper, 4 cups of dry white wine, 4 cups of water, salt

Method: 1. Put the pork fat and the goose fat in a braising pan, cover with water and simmer. Clean and dice the meat, the carrot and the onion. When the pork and goose fat have melted and the water has evaporated, add the meat, the carrot, the onion, the clove of garlic, the bouquet garni, and the white wine.
2. Cover and simmer for 4 hours. Then remove the lid from the pot, increase the heat slightly and stir until all the remaining liquid has completely evaporated. Remove the garlic and the bouquet garni.
3. Allow to cool until just warm, then lightly shred the meat with your hands and adjust the seasoning with salt and the green pepper.
4. Place the mixture in a terrine (or divide it between two terrines if more convenient), cover with a layer of melted lard and keep in the refrigerator for at least 2 days before serving.

5. Serve the terrine using a spoon to form into shell shapes, and garnish with green salad and naturally leavened bread.

Wines:

Lago di Caldaro Scelto
or Pelaverga

Marches-style goose terrine with black truffle sauce

Serves 6-8

1 young goose weighing about 6½ lb/3 kg, 2 tsp of isinglass (fish glue), 2½ oz/70 g white truffles, 2½ oz/70 g black truffles, salt, pepper, extra virgin oil
For the truffle sauce: 1 potato, 2½ oz/70 g white truffles, 1¾ oz/50 g black truffles, ¾ cup of chicken stock, extra virgin oil
For the garnish: 2 red tomatoes, 1 sprig of parsley, 1 bunch of young salad leaves

Method 1. Bone the goose, keeping only the central part of the back intact and cutting all the rest of the bird up into pieces, preferably large ones. Wash the liver with a little brandy. Soak the isinglass in cold water.
2. Arrange all the ingredients in a terrine, alternating layers of meat, white and black truffle cut into thin slices, the isinglass, oil, salt and pepper.
3. Vacuum seal the whole terrine and steam at 160°F/70°C until the temperature in the center reaches 150°F/65°C. Reduce the temperature to 40°F/5°C.
4. Prepare the sauce: clean the truffles and cut them into pieces, put all the ingredients in a vacuum sealed bag and cook at 205°F / 95°C for 60 minutes, then reduce the temperature to 40°F / 5°C. Whisk, and season with salt and pepper.

5. Parboil the tomatoes and dice them. Wash and drain the salad leaves.
6. Pour a thin layer of truffle sauce onto each plate, lay the salad leaves on top, arrange a slice of the terrine on them, surrounded with a garnish of tomato and parsley.

Note: This is a new look at a traditional recipe, using modern culinary technology.

Wines:

Verdicchio dei Castelli di Jesi Classico or
Reserve Terre di Franciacorta Chardonnay

STARTERS

Goose crackling

Serves 6-8

All the skin (and the fat) from one goose, sage, rosemary, 3 heads of red radicchio, 3-4 endive hearts, 2 small lettuces, the zest of ¼ of an orange, very finely shredded, 4 tsp extra virgin olive oil, good-quality vinegar to taste, a pinch of salt

Method: 1. Cut the skin into squares about 1 in/2 cm on a side and put them in a saucepan together with all the goose fat from the cavity and the rest of the bird. Add sage and rosemary and place on the lowest possible heat, stirring from time to time. Allow to cook until all the fat has been released and the pieces of skin have turned into crunchy crackling. Remove and drain well, and place on a double layer of kitchen paper to absorb the excess fat.
2. Wash the salad leaves, drain and chop into a salad bowl.
3. Dress with salt, vinegar and a little oil and arrange on plates, alternating with the shreds of orange zest. Place the crackling on top, and serve.

Wines:

*Extra dry Terre di Franciacorta
or Torrechiara Malmsey*

STARTERS

Squash flowers stuffed with goose liver

Serves 6

12 squash flowers, 10½ oz/300 g of goose liver, 3½ oz/100g of shallot, 10 tbsp of fresh ricotta,
1 oz/30 g of black truffle, 1 oz/30 g of carrot, 4 tsp of olive oil, pine kernels, fresh herbs, salt, pepper

Method: 1. Remove the pistils from the squash flowers and clean thoroughly, taking care not to damage them.
2. Stew the shallot in a frying pan for a few minutes, then sauté the liver, leaving it pink.
3. Remove from the heat and allow to cool, then blend in a food processor together with the ricotta.
4. Dice the carrots and boil for about 4 minutes, allow to cool in the water, and drain.

5. Finely dice the black truffle. Add the carrots and the truffle to the liver paste, put the paste into a piping bag and fill the squash flowers.
6. Steam the stuffed flowers for 4-5 minutes and serve with a pesto-style sauce made of pine kernels and fresh herbs.

Wines:

Istria Malmsey
or Fiano di Avellino

$$\boxed{\text{STARTERS}}$$

Tagliatelle with goose ragout and foie gras in coriander sauce

Serves 4

10½ oz/300 g fresh egg tagliatelle
For the ragout: 7 oz/200 g boned goose thigh, minced, 3½ oz/100 g pork loin, minced, 1 oz/30 g of pork fat, 2 cups/½ l of stock, 10½ oz/300 g of tomatoes,
1 oz/30 g of celery, 1 oz/30 g of onion, 1 oz/30 g of carrot, 1 glass of white wine, 6½ tbsp of extra virgin oil, salt and pepper to taste
For the sauce: 7 oz/200 g of goose foie gras, steamed, 6½ tbsp of goose stock (see recipe on page 52), 1 oz/30 g of white truffle, 1 tsp of ginger, 1 tsp of coriander

Method 1. Dice the celery, carrot and onion and brown them in pork fat; add the goose, the pork, the *foie gras* and continue to brown together. Add the glass of white wine and allow to evaporate. Add the tomato and 2 cups of stock and cook for about 45 minutes. Season with salt and pepper to taste.
2. Put all the ingredients for the sauce into a food processor and blend, then put the mixture through a fine sieve. Heat to 175°F/ 80°C.
3. Cook the tagliatelle *al dente* in plenty of boiling salted water. Drain and dress with the goose ragout.
4. To serve, pour a thin layer of sauce over the bottom of each plate and arrange the dressed tagliatelle on top.

Wines:

Sangiovese di Modigliana
or Solopaca di Castelvenere

Luigi Mariani

FIRST COURSES

Potato gnocchi with goose breast

Serves 4

10½ oz/300 g of potatoes, boiled, 5 tbsp of flour, the yolks of 2 eggs, 1 whole egg, ½ small glass of dry white grappa, a pinch of salt
For the sauce: 1 scallion, 1 knob of butter, 3½ oz/100 g of goose breast, 3½ oz/100 g of smoked goose breast,
2 tbsp gravy or cooking juices, 3 tbsp of cream

Method: 1. Peel the potatoes and mash them thoroughly. Add the flour, the egg yolks and whole egg, the grappa and a pinch of salt and mix to a thick, soft dough.
2. Leave the dough to stand for a few minutes, then cut it into gnocchi in the traditional way and press each one with the back of a fork. Cook the gnocchi in plenty of salted water.

3. To prepare the sauce, finely chop the scallion and fry it in the butter. Mince and add both the goose breasts and leave to cook for a few minutes. Pour over the gravy or cooking juices and half a ladle of stock and simmer for another 5 minutes. Add the cream and the gnocchi and allow to thicken for ½ minute. Pour into a warmed dish and serve.

Wines:

Dolcetto di Dogliani
or Santa Maddalena

FIRST COURSES

Miniature potato gnocchi with goose ragout

Serves 12

A generous 2 lb/1 kg of potatoes, 4 cups of flour, 6 eggs, 1 goose, salt to taste, 2 ribs of celery, 2 carrots, 2 onions, 1 bouquet garni, 2 cloves of garlic, 1 glass of good red wine, a generous 2 lb/1 kg of tomatoes, peeled, oil for frying, 12 leaves of Savoy cabbage

Method: 1. Peel and boil the potatoes, and mash or force them through a strainer. Knead the mashed potato with the flour, salt and eggs to form a firm, even dough. Roll out long sausages of dough and then cut these into pieces and roll the pieces one by one over the back of a grater.
2. Thoroughly clean the goose. Cut it into moderately sized pieces and brown in a frying pan with very little oil. This removes the excess fat.
3. Dice the celery, the carrot and the onion. Brown them in a little oil in a wide, low-sided pan together with the bouquet garni and the cloves of garlic, then immediately remove the garlic. Add the goose to the pan, pour over the wine and allow it to evaporate, then add the tomatoes. Gently simmer these ingredients until the goose is completely cooked. Remove the bouquet garni and when the goose has cooled, bone it. Mince the meat with a knife and put the cooking sauce through a vegetable mill.

Mix the sauce and minced meat together and boil for 5 minutes; season with salt and pepper to taste.
4. Cook the gnocchi in boiling salted water, draining them when they float back to the surface. Dress them with the very hot ragout.
5. Boil the cabbage leaves, no more than *al dente* (they should still be green). Place a leaf on each plate and arrange the dressed gnocchi on top; serve immediately.

Wines:

Pignolo di Buttrio
or Dolcetto di Diano

MAIN COURSES

Warm goose breast with watercress in balsamic vinegar dressing

Serves 4

½ goose breast, weighing about 14 oz/400 g, 2 cups/½ l of vegetable stock, 1 pomegranate, peeled, 2 tbsp of extra virgin olive oil, ½ glass of brandy, ⅓ cup/40 g of sultanas (previously soaked for 3 hours in water and brandy, 3 tbsp of pine kernels, shelled and roasted, 4 bunches of watercress, 1 tbsp vintage balsamic vinegar, salt and pepper to taste

Method: 1. Brown the goose breast on both sides over a high heat in a very little olive oil. Deglaze with the brandy and continue cooking in the oven at 355°F/180°C in a covered casserole dish, taking care to keep the breast covered to ⅓ of its thickness in vegetable stock at all times, until cooked as desired. (If the meat is preferred pink, it is advisable to remove it when the core temperature reaches 150°F/65°C).

2. Wash and drain the watercress and whisk together the oil with the balsamic vinegar and a little salt.

3. Arrange the watercress on plates and dress it with half the mixture of oil and vinegar. Cut the goose breast into slices while still warm and arrange on top of the watercress. Sprinkle with the pomegranate, the pine kernels and the sultanas and dress with the remaining oil and balsamic vinegar.

Wines:

*Collio Rosso di Cormons
or Pignocco Rosso*

Goose en croûte with braised cardoons and black truffle

Serves 6

1 goose, 1 lb 5 oz/600 g of cardoons, 5¼ oz/150 g of truffle, ¾ cup of extra virgin oil, 5¼ oz/150 g of puff pastry, 3½ tbsp of butter, 1¾ oz/50 g of pork caul, 3 ½ oz/100 g of mixed vegetables, ¾ cup of red wine, stock, 1 tomato, 1 bouquet garni

Method: 1. Joint the goose, separating the breasts, the thighs and the liver. Use the carcass to make the stock (*see* recipe on page 52).

2. Divide the breast into two, then cut into pieces of the desired size.

3. Blend the liver and some of the truffle in a food processor. Bone the thighs and stuff them with the liver and truffle mixture, then wrap them in the pork caul.

4. Braise the cardoons with a little oil, a few slices of truffle, and a little stock.

5. Quickly brown the breasts in very hot oil and allow to cool. Roll out the puff pastry, wrap the goose breasts in it and cook in a pre-heated oven at 430°F/220°C for 6-8 minutes.

7. Slice the thighs into cutlets. Arrange the cardoons on plates, followed by the thigh cutlets and the breast pieces. Thicken the cooking juices with the butter and drizzle over each plate.

Wines:

*Sassella Riserva
or Aglianico del Taburno*

Marinated goose breast with duck liver and balsamic vinegar

Serves 4

2 goose breasts, each weighing a generous 10oz/300 g, 5 oz/150 g of duck liver, 3½ oz/100 g of pork caul, the white of 1 egg, 1½ oz/40 g of carrot, 1½ oz/40 g of zucchini, 1½ oz/40 g yellow capsicum, 1½ oz/40 g of celery, white breadcrumbs, 4 tsp of clarified butter
For the marinade: ¾ oz/20 g of carrot, ¾ oz/20 g of celery, ¾ oz/20 g of onion, 1 cup of sweet white wine, 10 tsp of salt, ⅓ oz of fresh oregano, ⅓ oz of fresh thyme
For the sauce: 6½ tbsp of balsamic vinegar, 1 oz/30 g of scallion, 1¼ cups of goose stock (see recipe on page 52)

Method: 1. Boil together all the ingredients for the marinade. When it has cooled, macerate the goose breasts in the liquid for 12 hours.
2. Finely dice the carrot, celery, capsicum and green part of the zucchini; blanch them and allow to cool. Clean and mince the duck liver and add the egg white, the vegetables, the salt, the pepper and some of the breadcrumbs (enough to substantially thicken the mixture).
3. Remove the breasts from the marinade and drain them. Cut them in half and spread them all over with the liver paste; then wrap them one by one in the pork caul. Clarify the butter in an ovenproof pan, quickly brown the breasts and then roast at 355°F/180°C for 7-8 minutes. Leave the breasts to stand for 5 minutes, keeping them warm.
4. Prepare the sauce: finely shred the scallion, skim the fat off the cooking juices from the pan the breasts were cooked in, and add the balsamic vinegar and the scallion. Reduce and add the stock. Mix to a creamy consistency and whisk in a knob of butter.
5. Slice the breasts into cutlets, arrange them in a fan shape on each plate and coat them with the sauce. Serve with vegetables glazed with whisked oil (for example, carrots and zucchini cut into attractive shapes, parboiled in salted water then simmered in stock in a frying pan; the oil is added when they are completely cooked).

Wines:

Santa Maddalena di Obermoserhof
or Aglianico di Santa Croce

Goose soufflé with sweet-and-sour onions and cloves

Makes 15 soufflés

For the béchamel sauce: 3½ tbsp/50 g of butter, 5 tsp/50 g of flour, 1 cup/250 ml of milk
For the soufflé base: 3½ tbsp/50 g of sheep's milk ricotta, 1¾ oz/50 g of creamed or mashed potato, 1¾ oz / 50 g of mild cheese, grated,
the yolks of 4 eggs, the whites of 4 eggs, whisked until stiff, 5¼ oz/150 g goose purée (see below), salt and pepper to taste
For the sweet-and-sour onions and cloves: 10½ oz/300 g of small onions, 6½ tbsp/100 g of sugar, 3½ tbsp/50ml of balsamic vinegar,
15 cloves, 1 sprig of rosemary, 1 bay leaf

Method: 1. To make the goose purée, stew together 2 carrots, 1 rib of celery, 1 onion, a generous 1 lb/500 g of lean goose meat (the thighs can also be used) and as much stock as required. When this is cooked, whisk and sieve it.

2. To make the sweet-and-sour onions and cloves, put all the ingredients, except the onions, into a cooking pot and bring to a boil. Peel and add the onions, and cook for about 10 minutes.

3. To make the soufflé base, grate or finely chop the cheese. Prepare the béchamel sauce. When it has cooled add the ricotta, the creamed or mashed potato, the grated cheese, the goose purée and the egg yolks. Mix all these ingredients together and fold in the egg whites. Season with salt and pepper to taste.

4. Grease small individual molds and line them with a coating of breadcrumbs. Fill the mold with the soufflé mixture, and bake at 355°F/180°C for 15 minutes.

5. Arrange the onions and cloves with their sauce in soup plates. Turn out each soufflé onto a bed of onion and cloves and serve immediately.

Wines:

Terre Rosse Pinot bianco di Zola Predosa
or Rosato di Alezio

MAIN COURSES

Goose mountain-style

Serves 8

1 young goose weighing about 4½ lb/2 kg, 3½ oz/100 g raw prosciutto, in a single piece, 4 sage leaves,
¾ cup of white wine, oil for frying, pepper, freshly grated nutmeg, salt
For the accompaniment: 2 red cabbages, 3½ tbsp of butter, 2 apples, 1 onion, the juice of 1 lemon, 1 tbsp of apple purée,
⅔ cup/50 ml of balsamic vinegar, salt

Method: 1. Clean the goose, removing some of the fat, and cut it into small pieces. Season with the pepper, nutmeg and salt.

2. Brown the goose in a little oil in an ovenproof pan over a high heat.

3. Sprinkle over the white wine, allow to evaporate, then add the piece of prosciutto and the sage. Roast at 390°F/200°C for 1 hour and 15 minutes, depending on the weight of the goose.

4. When the goose is cooked, remove it to a serving dish. Dice the prosciutto and sprinkle it over the goose.

5. Skim the fat off the cooking juices and pour them, very hot, over the goose and prosciutto. Serve immediately with an accompaniment of red cabbage, prepared as follows:

Method (accompaniment): 1. Cut the cabbage into strips. Gently heat the butter in a pan until it foams, add the strips of cabbage and the apple purée and cook over a moderate heat, stirring from time to time.

2. Peel and slice the apples and chop the onion. Add the apple, the chopped onion, the lemon juice and the vinegar. Add salt to taste and continue cooking until the apples and vegetables are cooked.

Wines:

Carema
or Rosso di Montepulciano

MAIN COURSES

Goose with sour apples

Serves 8

1 Padua goose weighing about 8¾ lb/4 kg, 1¼ cups/300 g of butter, ⅔ cup/150 ml of extra virgin olive oil, ¾ cup/200 ml of dry white wine
For the stuffing: 4 green Granny Smith apples, the liver of the goose, 10½ oz/300 g of duck liver, 7 oz/200 g of veal, 3½ oz/100 g of bacon,
3 bread rolls softened in milk, the yolk of 2 eggs, 4 shallots (chopped),1 green apple to garnish

Method: 1. Clean the goose, taking care to remove and reserve any lumps of fat from inside the body cavity. Sear the goose, season the cavity with salt and pepper.

2. Prepare the stuffing. Peel and slice the apples and sauté them with a knob of butter in a non-stick frying pan and set aside.

3. Separately, sauté together the goose and duck livers, the veal, the bacon and the shallot, then blend them in a food processor. Thoroughly crumble up and add the bread, and the egg yolks. Finally, add the apple.

4. Stuff the goose with this mixture and sew up the opening with kitchen twine so that the stuffing will not come out during cooking.

5. In an ovenproof dish, brown the goose well on both sides in butter and oil (or in the goose fat removed earlier).

6. Roast at 355°F/180°C for 50 minutes then at 390°F/200°C for a further 40 minutes. Then turn off the oven but leave the goose in for 20 minutes more. While cooking, baste the goose from time to time with the white wine; baste the breast only with the fat that trickles from the goose and collects in the bottom of the pan.

7. Carve the breast and thighs into thin slices and serve with a scoop of stuffing garnished with slices of green apple.

Wines:

Traminer Friulano
or Donnaz

MAIN COURSES

Goose with chestnut stuffing

Serves 6-8

1 goose weighing about 4½ lb/2 kg, 14 oz/400 g of veal, 3 large sausages, 10½ oz/300 g of fresh sweet chestnuts, 1 glass of white wine, 1 cup of breadcrumbs, softened in milk and gently squeezed out, butter, salt and pepper to taste

Method: 1. Boil and peel the chestnuts, leaving them whole. (Dried chestnuts can also be used after soaking in warm water for about 3 hours).
2. For the stuffing, mince the veal and the sausages and season with salt and pepper. Add the breadcrumbs and the chestnuts.
3. Bone the goose (*see* page 51) and stuff it with this mixture, sewing up the opening and trussing the whole goose with twine. Spread butter over the goose and roast it at 355°F/180°C for about 1 hour, basting it occasionally with wine.

4. Carve the goose into slices while it is still hot and serve with its cooking juices.

Wines:

*Cabernet di Breganze
or Rosso di Premaor*

MAIN COURSES

Goose breast with crab apples and prunes

Serves 4

1 goose breast, 4 crab apples (or 2 green apples), 2 cups of goose stock (see recipe on page 52), 1 glass of white wine, 8 prunes, pitted, 8 rashers of smoked bacon, 1 tbsp of olive oil, 1 knob of butter, a little stale bread, fresh horseradish

Method: 1. Divide the goose breast into its two parts and clean them but leave most of the skin on. Season with salt and pepper.

2. Fry the goose breast in a very little oil, skin side down, browning the meat well but keeping it rare. Set aside some of the fat from the meat and discard the rest. Pour over the white wine, allow to evaporate and add the stock. Keep warm, taking care that the breasts do not become overcooked.

3. Wash, peel and dice the apples, and dice the bread. Sauté them together in a little goose fat.

4. Wrap each prune in a rasher of bacon and brown in a hot oven.

5. Carve the goose breasts into slices and arrange them in a fan shape on individual plates. Reduce and strain the sauce, thicken it with a knob of butter, and pour over the goose slices. Garnish each plate with a tablespoonful of apple and bread and two prunes wrapped in bacon. Grate fresh horseradish on top, and serve.

Wines:

*Merlot di Premariacco
or Rossese di Dolceacqua*

MAIN COURSES

Goose breast with shallots and mostarda

Serves 4

1 whole goose breast weighing about 12oz/350 g, 2 shallots, ½ cup good-quality wine vinegar, 1 tbsp demi-glaze (or concentrated stock), ½ cup water, 2 oz/60 g mostarda di fruta (glacé fruits), diced, salt, pepper, ½ stock cube

Method: 1. Divide the goose breast into its two parts and remove the fat and skin from both sides.

2. Cut 1 tbsp of goose fat into thin strips and melt it in a copper pan; when it begins to brown, add the two pieces of breast meat and brown them on both sides over a low heat for about 4-5 minutes so that the meat remains pink in the middle when cooked; remove from the frying pan and leave to stand for a few minutes.

3. Meanwhile, prepare the sauce. Finely chop the shallot, put it into the pan and fry gently for a moment, then pour over the vinegar. Reduce until almost all the liquid has evaporated, then add the demi-glaze and the water. Remove the sauce, and season to taste with salt, pepper, and the stock cube.

4. Season the breasts with salt and pepper, carve them into slices and arrange on plates with the mostarda on top.

Wines:

Merlot di Pinzano al Tagliamento or Carmignano Rosso

MAIN COURSES

Salad of goose breast with orange zest

Serves 4

*2 goose breasts, with their skin, 1 orange, 1 bunch of young green salad leaves, 1 tbsp balsamic vinegar,
extra virgin oil, salt and pepper to taste*

Method: 1. Remove the skin from the breasts and cut it into fine ribbons.
2. Pour a trickle of oil into a high-sided pan or shallow casserole dish and sauté the breasts, browning them on both sides; then salt and pepper them and roast at 355°F/180°C for about 10 minutes. Remove from the oven, wrap in foil, and leave to stand, keeping warm, for 20 minutes. This gives the meat an attractive pink color.
3. Peel the orange, finely shred the zest into a julienne and parboil in water, then cool. Squeeze the juice from the orange.
4. Remove all the fat from the pan and return it to the heat. Deglaze with balsamic vinegar, add the orange juice and the zest, allow to reduce slightly, and remove from the heat.
5. Separately, in a high-sided pan or shallow casserole dish, sauté the ribbons of skin over a high heat, and salt them.

6. Wash the salad leaves and drain well.
7. Place the salad leaves in the center of each plate, and dress with salt, oil and balsamic vinegar. Carve the breasts into thin slices and arrange them in a sunburst around the salad; pour over the glaze, garnish with the hot crackling and serve.

Wines:

*Terre di Franciacorta
or Rosato del Salento*

MAIN COURSES

Stuffed roast goose

Serves 6-8

1 young goose weighing 6½ lb/3 kg to 8¾ lb/4 kg, 1¾ lb/800 g of Veneto headcheese, 3½ oz/100 g of green olives, pitted,
20 roast chestnuts, the yolks of 2 eggs, 2 Norcia black truffles, salt, pepper, ½ a nutmeg, 2 onions, 1 rib of celery,
2 carrots, 3 cloves of garlic, 1 sprig of sage, 1¼ cups/300 ml of Marsala

Method: 1. Choose a plump young goose with fine skin. Pluck, and draw it, setting aside the liver. Cut off the webbed part of the feet, the head and the neck 4½ in/10 cm from the body. Make a cut in the back of the bird reaching as far as the thighs, removing the neck bone and the wishbone. Cut the wing tips and the neck into small pieces.
2. Prepare the stuffing. Knead together the headcheese, the liver, and the egg yolks with salt and pepper. Peel and add the whole chestnuts; add the olives; chop and add the truffles. Season the goose with salt and pepper; stuff it, and securely sew up the opening in the back.
3. Put the goose into a large oval casserole dish (preferably enameled cast iron, with a lid). Chop the vegetables and arrange them on top of the goose; cut up the bones and put them around the goose. Cover with the lid, but leave an opening for the steam to escape. Roast at 390°F/200°C for

2-3 hours (depending on the size of the goose). When the goose is browned, lift it out of the casserole dish. Keep warm.
4. Return the casserole dish to the heat and pour over the Marsala, dissolving all the cooking juices; strain the resulting sauce. (Meanwhile, the goose will have cooled down a little and will be easier to carve.) Carve the breast lengthwise, alternating slices of breast and of meat with stuffing. Pour over the sauce and serve.

Wines:

Cabernet di Capriva
or Rosso di Franciacorta

STARTERS

Stuffed neck of goose

Serves 4

4 goose necks, 4 tbsp of fresh pistachios, 2 oz/60 g of Norcia black truffle, 3½ oz/100 g of early vegetables (such as zucchini, carrots, asparagus, small onions, peas, green beans and squash), 4oz/120 g of goose breast and thigh meat, extra virgin olive oil, thyme, salt and pepper to taste, 2 tsp of balsamic vinegar, 1 bunch of young green salad leaves

Method: 1. Thoroughly clean and bone the goose necks.

2. Brown the goose breast and thigh meat in a frying pan with the olive oil and thyme. Mince the meat with a knife or in a mincer.

3. Dice the vegetables and sauté them in the frying pan.

4. Parboil the pistachios and shell them.

5. Chop the truffle into small pieces. Add the vegetables, the chopped truffle and the pistachios to the meat. Season this stuffing with salt and pepper to taste, and fill the goose necks with it, using a piping bag. Tie the necks up at both ends and wrap them in cellophane film.

6. Steam them in the oven for 8 minutes, then remove the film and cook in a frying pan for a further 5 minutes.

7. Allow to cool until just warm, cut into slices and arrange on a bed of salad leaves. Just before serving, dress with balsamic vinegar.

Wines:

Cesanese del Piglio
or Merlot del Lazio di Montefalcone

MAIN COURSES

Goose thigh with Savoy cabbage

Serves 4

4 goose thighs, extra virgin olive oil, 1 clove of garlic, 1 medium-sized Savoy cabbage, tomato purée, salt and pepper to taste

Method: 1. Finely chop the garlic and gently fry it in the olive oil in a large casserole dish. Add the thighs and brown them on both sides. Reduce the heat and finish cooking the meat.

2. Meanwhile, coarsely cut the cabbage and parboil it for about 10 minutes in plenty of salted water.

3. Strain the cabbage, add it to the meat, and continue cooking for about 1 hour. Season with salt and pepper to taste, and serve.

Wines:

*Barbera Oltrepò
or Dolcetto di Ovada*

MAIN COURSES

Griddled goose breast

Serves 4

*2 goose breasts each weighing about 12 oz/350 g, 2 cloves of garlic, 2 bay leaves, white wine ,
1 tbsp butter, ½ tbsp flour, salt, pepper*

Method: 1. Wrap the goose breasts in aluminum foil, each one with a clove of garlic and a bay leaf. Bake at 480°F/250°C for 15 minutes.

2. Open the foil and set aside the liquid and the bay leaves and garlic. Arrange the breasts skin side down on a griddle and cook over a very low heat for about 10 minutes until the skin is well browned, then turn over and cook for a further 2 minutes.

3. Meanwhile, prepare the sauce. Put the liquid and the bay leaves and garlic into a frying pan, add a little white wine, and the butter and flour. Stir well and cook to a smooth sauce. Remove the bay leaves and garlic.

4. Finely slice the breasts, arrange them on each plate, pour over the sauce and serve with potatoes roasted in goose fat.

Wines:

*Barbera d'Asti
or Aglianico del Vulture*

MAIN COURSES

Goose breast with stewed squash and black truffles

Serves 4

2 goose breasts, each weighing about 10 oz/300 g, 2 oz/60 g Norcia black truffle, thinly sliced, a generous 1 lb of squash, peeled and cut into slices, 3½ tbsp/50 ml of extra virgin olive oil, ¼ cup/60 ml of red wine, 2 tbsp/30 g of butter, 1 tsp/5 ml of balsamic vinegar, salt, freshly ground pepper, a few sprigs of parsley to garnish

Method: 1. Macerate the goose breasts in the oil and red wine for about 30 minutes.

2. Drain the meat, season with salt and pepper, and brown on both sides over a high heat. Place in the oven at 390°F/200°C until the meat is cooked; the fatty part should be crisp.

3. Meanwhile, stew the squash in a little olive oil and water, and when it is soft season with salt.

4. Boil the cooking juices from the meat, add the balsamic vinegar and mix in the butter. Reduce very slightly and season with salt and pepper.

5. Arrange the squash in a serving dish. Carve the goose breasts into thin slices and arrange them on the squash. Pour over the sauce and garnish with the black truffle and parsley.

Wines:

*Merlot dell'Alto Mincio
or Cirò Superiore*

Roast goose with raisin and foie gras stuffing

Serves 4

1 small goose weighing about 4 lb/1.8 kg, ¼ cup/50 g of raisins, 3½ tbsp of port, 1¾ oz/50 g of brown bread, 1¾ oz/50 g white bread, 3½ oz/100 g of goose foie gras,
¼ cup of walnuts, chopped, 3½ oz/100g of chicken breast, nutmeg, 4 tbsp of extra virgin olive oil, 3 cloves, 5 juniper berries, salt, freshly ground pepper

Method: 1. Wash and dry the goose. Carefully remove the skin, working slowly from the neck, so that it can be stuffed without the skin tearing.
2. Soak the raisins in the port for about 30 minutes.
3. Finely dice the white and brown bread and the *foie gras* and mix them together in a small pan over a low heat. Add the walnuts. Drain and add the raisins. In a separate pan, reduce the port to a syrup then add it to the other ingredients.
4. Put the chicken meat into a food processor and blend it to a smooth paste on a high-speed setting. Add salt, pepper and nutmeg, and mix into the stuffing. Thoroughly mix all the ingredients. Pre-heat the oven to 375°F/190°C.
5. Fill the goose with this stuffing and sew up the opening with kitchen twine.

6. Heat the oil in a large pan and brown the goose on both sides, taking care not to break the stitches when turning it. Add the cloves and the juniper. Cover the pan and cook for about 70-80 minutes in a low oven, adding a little water from time to time.
7. Remove the goose and carve into portions. Skim the fat off the cooking juices, reduce a little and pour over the pieces of goose.

Wines:

Lagrein Dukel Riserva
or Portulano di Alezio

Goose with pepper sauce

Serves 8-10

1 goose weighing about 6½ lb/3 kg, 1 glass dry white wine , about 4 cups/1 l chicken stock, 1 bunch of rosemary and sage, 1 clove of garlic,
salt, freshly ground white pepper, olive oil, a generous knob of butter
For the pepper sauce: the goose liver (or 12¼ oz/350 g chicken livers, thoroughly cleaned), 3½ oz/100 g Veneto headcheese (if not available, replace with salami),
½ glass white wine, about 1 glass chicken stock, 1 onion, 1 clove of garlic, the zest of 1 lemon, about 1 oz/30 g breadcrumbs, parsley, chopped, 3 anchovy fillets,
1 oz/30 g capers, ¾ oz/20 g grated ginger root, the juice of 1 lemon, a few drops of vinegar, oil, butter, salt, pepper

Methods: 1. Clean the goose; put the garlic, rosemary, and sage inside it; season with salt and pepper. Heat the olive oil in a high-sided pan or casserole dish, melt the knob of butter and brown the goose evenly, over a moderate heat. Remove from the pan, skim off the fat, and deglaze the cooking juices with a glass of dry white wine and some chicken stock. Put the goose back into the dish and continue cooking in the oven at 355°F/ 180°c for 1 hour 45 minutes or 2 hours. Baste from time to time with chicken stock, so the bottom of the casserole dish never dries out.
2. While the goose is cooking, prepare the sauce. Chop the onion, crush the garlic, and chop the headcheese. Brown the onion and the garlic in a little oil; add the chicken livers and the headcheese. Cook for a few minutes, then pour over a little white wine and chicken stock. Add the anchovies, chopped capers, ginger root, and chopped lemon zest. Simmer

for at least 20 minutes, then add the lemon juice and a few drops of vinegar. Thicken with breadcrumbs and finally add the parsley.
3. Carve the goose into pieces, arrange in a pan, and cover with the pepper sauce. Simmer together for 3–4 minutes so that all the flavours are absorbed, and serve. Yellow polenta is the ideal accompaniment for this dish, especially cut into slices and toasted on a griddle; it is also excellent with sweet-and-sour baby onions.

Wines:

Teroldego
or Valpolicella di Ripasso

Goose breast en croûte with parsley, in a grappa sauce

Serves 4

2 goose breasts, 4 sheets of filo pastry
For the garnish: 4 beef tomatoes, 12 raspberries, 4 sprigs of redcurrants, 4 strawberries, 4 porcini mushrooms, 12 honey fungus caps, 2 chanterelle mushrooms,
1 tsp/5 g shallot, a pinch/5 g savory, 4 figs, 4 segments of quince, 1 tbsp/15 g extra virgin olive oil
For the parsley filling: 1¾ oz/50 g sandwich loaf, 6½ tbsp/100 g butter, 1 oz/20 g parsley, a pinch of garlic, a pinch of basil
For the stock: 1 oz/20 g shallot, a pinch of rosemary, 1 oz/2o g celery, 4 tsp/20 g butter, 9 oz/250 g goose bones, 6½ tbsp/100 ml vegetable stock, 1 clove of garlic,
3½ tbsp/50 ml grappa, 2 tbsp/30 ml black grape juice

Method: 1. Prepare the parsley filling: put all the ingredients in a food processor and blend to a creamy paste.
2. Dress the goose breast, season with salt, pepper, and oil, and brown in the frying pan until the fatty side is very crunchy.
3. Make a cut under the skin and stuff it with the parsley paste, then replace the skin and wrap in the filo pastry. Brush with melted butter and cook in a pre-heated oven at 375°F/190°C for about 12 minutes.
4. Roast the bones with the butter and seasoning, deglaze with the strawberry grape juice and stock, and reduce. Sieve the sauce, add the grappa and adjust the seasoning to taste.
5. Chop the shallot. Fry all the mushrooms in the oil, with the shallot, savory, salt, and pepper. Make a cut in the porcini caps with a pastry cutter and stuff the chanterelles and honey fungus inside.

6. Caramelize the slices of quince and the figs in a frying pan with a little butter. Peel the tomatoes, cut out the insides and stuff them with raspberries, redcurrants and black grapes.
7. Arrange a stuffed tomato, a porcini cap, a fig and the caramelized quince on each plate together with two slices of goose breast, pour over the sauce, and serve.

Wines:

Pinot Nero Alto Adige
or Essenza di Faedo

MAIN COURSES

Goose breast in apple vinegar with baby onions

Serves 4

2 goose breasts with their fat, weighing a generous 2 pounds/1 kg, 7 oz/200 g baby onions, peeled, 4 pippins, ½ glass apple vinegar, 4 cups/1 l stock, 4 bay leaves, salt, freshly ground black pepper

Method: 1. Remove the fat from the breasts, dice it and melt it down in a saucepan over a low heat.

2. Remove any remaining skin and flour the breasts on both sides; brown them in the goose fat for a few minutes, add the whole peeled baby onions and cook until they are a light hazelnut colour.

3. Peel and slice the apples. Remove the cooking fat and add the apple slices and the bay leaves; cook for a few minutes and add the vinegar, allow to evaporate, add the stock and cook in the oven at 355°F/ 180°C for about 30 minutes. Season with salt and pepper to taste.

4. When the meat is cooked, remove the breasts and carve them into very thin slices; fan these out on individual plates and pour over the apple and onion sauce. Garnish with bay leaves and serve immediately.

Wines:

Sangiovese Superiore or Fiorano Rosso

MAIN COURSES

Goose casserole with Savoy cabbage and polenta

Serves 8

1 goose, weighing about 8¾ lb/4 kg, 3½ oz/100 g pork rind, cut into small sticks and parboiled for 5 minutes, 1 clove of garlic, 2 onions, 1 carrot, 2 ribs of celery, 1 glass dry white wine, 1 Savoy cabbage, fairly large, 3½ tbsp/50 g butter, 2 tbsp extra virgin olive oil, 8½ cups/2 l vegetable stock, salt, pepper, 1 tsp chopped parsley, 1 small tomato, blanched, peeled and seeded

Method: 1. Clean the Savoy cabbage, separate the leaves and remove the thickest ribs, then parboil for 1 minute. Clean, wash and chop the onions, carrots, and celery into thin sticks. Clean the goose, remove the skin and carve it into fairly small pieces; salt and flour the pieces lightly.
2. Heat 4 tsp of butter and the oil in a saucepan; add the clove of garlic, brown it and remove; then add the vegetables and brown them gently.
3. When the vegetables are well browned, add the pork rind and the goose meat and stew for 10 minutes; pour over the white wine, chop and add the tomato.
4. Allow the mixture to almost dry out, then add the vegetable stock, cover, and simmer over a low heat. After half an hour, add the Savoy cabbage and leave to cook for at least another 45 minutes.
5. Check that the ingredients are cooked, season with salt and pepper to taste, sprinkle with the chopped parsley and serve very hot. Accompany with piping hot polenta.

Wines:
*Barbera del Monferrato
or Raboso di Campodipietra*

Goose sausage with crawfish

Serves 6-7

Salted lamb entrails, 1 young goose, 2 glasses red wine, robust and full-bodied, 4 cloves of garlic, sage, black pepper,
juniper berries, fine sea salt, 10½ oz/300 g fresh streaky bacon, 1 tbsp Parmesan, generous 2 lbs/1 kg crawfish, 2 glasses/½ l dry white wine, 1 onion,
2 leeks, 2 carrots, 2 stalks of celery, 1 potato, bayleaf, thyme, parsley, 1 porcini cap, 2 cups/½ l cream
Garnish: thyme and chervil

Method: 1. Wash the lamb entrails and macerate it for 12 hours in red wine and water with 2 cloves of garlic and sage.

2. Chop 2 cloves of garlic and macerate them in the red wine for 2 hours.

3. Skin and bone the goose. Make a stock from the carcass and onion, carrot, and celery browned in the oven.

4. Coarsely mince 1½ lb/700 g goose meat and 10½ oz/300 g bacon, and season with salt, pepper, and a little crushed juniper. Sieve the garlic-flavoured wine. Mince the stuffing again on medium, and season with the wine, a little stock, and Parmesan. Knead well by hand, then leave to stand for 12 hours. Shape into 12–14 sausages with a sausage machine.

5. Make a bouillon with water, wine, thyme, leek and bay leaf. When it boils, toss in the crawfish and boil for 1 minute. Drain, set aside the liquid and clean the crawfish tails. Grind the shells in a mortar. Make a sauce with 4 cups/1 l of crawfish stock, white wine, 2 chopped tomatoes, and cream; boil for 30 minutes. Strain, return to the heat and reduce by half to give the sauce a syrupy consistency. Dice 1 leek, the potato, 1 carrot, 1 rib of celery, and the porcini. Blanch in salted water and mix into the sauce.

6. Brown the sausages in oil with the bay leaf and bake in the oven at 390°F/ 200°C for 20 minutes. They should remain pink inside. Slice and arrange on the plate, interspersed with crawfish tails, and sprinkle over some sauce. Garnish with sprigs of thyme and chervil.

Wines:

*Oltrepò Riserva di Montalto
or Lacrima di Morro d'Alba*

MAIN COURSES

Roast goose breast with caramelized vegetables in balsamic vinegar

Serves ten

3 goose breasts, 2 zucchini, 1 egg-plant, 1 yellow capsicum, 7 oz/200 g celeriac, 2 artichokes, 1 rib of Florence fennel , ½ a head of broccoli, 3 baby onions, 4 cloves of garlic, 3 sprigs of thyme, 7 tsp/35 g cane sugar, 2 tbsp/30 ml balsamic vinegar, 2 tbsp/30 ml white wine, 2 tbsp/30 ml cognac, 3½ tbsp/50 g butter, 4½ tbsp/70 ml extra virgin olive oil

Method: 1. Dice the carrot, celery, and zucchini, and boil in salted water; drain and allow to cool. Clean the artichokes, and cook them in acidulated water with a little oil. Dice the capsicum and blanch in boiling water. Cut the broccoli into florets and boil them. Boil the Florence fennel, then dice it. Dice the egg-plant and sauté it in the frying pan with a little extra virgin oil. Boil the baby onions and then dice them. When all the vegetables are cooked, mix them together and set aside.

2. Remove excess fat from the goose breasts, salt and pepper them well, and brown them in a casserole dish with a little oil, the thyme and the unpeeled garlic. Continue cooking in the oven at 355°F/180°C for about 8 minutes; the meat should remain rare.

3. Leave the meat to stand while keeping hot for at least 5 minutes; sauté the vegetables in a frying pan with a little butter. When they are piping hot, sprinkle them with the cane sugar and pour over the balsamic vinegar; allow to evaporate, add the cognac and the white wine, dissolving the sugar, and finally add a little extra virgin oil.

4. Carve the goose breasts into slices and arrange them on the plates; place the caramelized vegetables on top with some of the juice that has formed, and serve.

Wines:

*Grattammacco Rosso
or San Colombano Banino Rosso superiore*

Stuffed goose

Serves 10-12

1 goose, weighing about 13 lb 2 oz/6 kg to 15 lbs 5 oz/7 kg (I cook geese starting at the end of December, when they are really mature).
For the stuffing: generous 2 lb/1 kg lean pork, 10½ oz/300 g terrine of foie gras, 10½ oz/300 g white bacon fat, 1 tube of truffle paste, 5¼ oz/150 g brioche,
spices (a freshly ground mixture of black Jamaican pepper (allspice), white pepper, cardamom, cinnamon, and Szechwan pepper), 2 tbsp very good brandy
For braising: 2 carrots, 2 white onions, 2 ribs green celery, 1 bulb of garlic, 1 leek, 1 bunch of aromatic herbs (thyme, rosemary, sage, parsley, chives),
generous 1 lb/500 g ripe tomatoes or canned peeled tomatoes, 1 bottle good quality sparkling wine (remember that even for cooking only good quality
wine should be used), 4 cups/1 l unsalted chicken stock, 6½ tbsp/100 ml olive oil, 3½ oz/100 g butter, salt, spices

Method: 1. Completely bone the goose starting from the back, and set aside the carcass. Mince the meat together with the bacon fat, cut the *foie gras* into pieces and force through a sieve, soak the brioche in a little sparkling wine and squeeze it out well, and mix together all the ingredients for the stuffing; season with salt and spices. Lay out the goose on a chopping board and stuff it, then sew it up with kitchen twine.
2. Put half the oil and 3½ tbsp/50 g butter into a braising pan; half the garlic, clean and dice all the vegetables (except the tomatoes), and chop up the goose carcass; gently fry the garlic and all the vegetables (except the tomatoes) with the goose carcass to make a *mirepoix*. While the vegetables are cooking, brown the goose in a large frying pan with the remaining fat, turning it continuously until well browned. Remove it from the fat and put it into the braising pan with the vegetables, keeping the

heat high; add the remaining wine, boil to evaproate the alcohol, chop up the tomatoes and then add the stock with the aromatic herbs and chopped tomatoes. Skim the fat and froth from the stock. Cover and cook over a low heat for 2½ hours. When it is cooked, remove the goose, strain the stock and reduce it slightly over a low heat to make a sauce.
3. Carve the goose into thick slices, glaze it with the sauce and serve extremely hot accompanied with boiled spinach.

Wines:

Barbaresco
or Brunello di Montalcino

MAIN COURSES

Goose with fruit stuffing

Serves 6

1 young goose, weighing about 4½ lb/2 kg, 2 cloves of garlic, 3 apples, 3½ oz/100 g prunes, 4 tbsp breadcrumbs, 1 egg, 1 tbsp sugar, salt

Method: 1. Rub the goose all over, inside and out, with garlic and salt. The flavors are even better if the goose is macerated in the wine, salt and garlic for twenty-four hours before cooking.

2. Pit the prunes and boil them quickly with a cup of water. Grate the apples and thoroughly mix the grated apple, the cooked prunes, the breadcrumbs, the egg, and the sugar. This mixture can be moistened with red wine and a little salt added to taste.

3. Stuff the goose with this mixture and sew up the opening. Spread it well with fat all over, and place in the oven, which should be preheated to a high temperature (at least 390°F/ 200°C). Cook for about two hours, basting with its own fat from time to time during cooking.

4. Allow the meat to stand for about 20 minutes before serving.

5. Arrange a slice of breast, and a slice of thigh on each plate, with a spoonful of stuffing beside them.

Wines:

Schioppettino di Cialla
or Mantua Ancellotta

Roast goose breast with arbutus honey in a balsamic vinegar sauce

Serves two

12¼ oz/350 g goose breast, just under 1 tbsp/20 g arbutus (strawberry tree) honey, 1⅔ cups/400 ml balsamic vinegar, ¾ cup/200 ml extra virgin olive oil, 2 segments of shallot, 1¾ oz/50 g potato, 2 sprigs of tarragon, 1 large Golden Delicious apple, 4 tsp/20 g superfine sugar

Method: 1. Salt and pepper the goose breast, give it a sheen of honey all over and brown it quickly in a dry non-stick frying pan. Fast-cool it.
2. Vacuum-pack the goose breast in an oven-proof envelope or bag; steam in a "three-way" oven at 130°F/55°C and stop cooking when the temperature in the middle of the goose breast reaches 120°F/50°C. Fast-cool and then set aside in the refrigerator.
3. Peel the apple, cut into 12 segments and vacuum-pack it in an oven-proof envelope or bag. Steam in a "three-way" oven at 195°F/90°C for 10–12 minutes. Fast-cool and then set aside in the refrigerator.
4. Peel and slice the shallot and potato. Pour the balsamic vinegar into a saucepan and place on a low heat with 1 sprig of tarragon, the shallot and the potato; reduce the liquid over to about half its volume and then whisk up with the oil.

5. Re-heat the goose breast but do not allow the temperature at the centre to exceed 120°F/ 50°C. Sprinkle the apple with sugar and caramelize it.
6. Cut the breast into escalopes and serve on a large, heated plate; garnish with the slices of caramelized apple, and finally strain and pour over the vinegar sauce.
NB: This recipe is a demonstration of how to use the latest culinary technology, from vacuum-packing to the "three-way" oven and fastcooler.

Wines:

*Late-harvest Italian Terre Rosse Riesling
or Rossese di Dolceacqua*

MAIN COURSES

$\mathcal{S}$weet-and-sour goose thighs

Serves 4

*4 medium-sized goose thighs, ¾ cup/200 ml balsamic vinegar, 2¾ oz/80 g candied raisins, 6 tbsp/40 g pine kernels, 1½ oz/40 g plain chocolate,
6½ tbsp/100 ml extra virgin olive oil, 1¼ cups/300 ml roux, 1¾ oz/50 g thyme, 1¾ oz/50 g rosemary, 2 cloves of garlic, 6½ tbsp/100 g butter,
1¼ cups/300 ml red wine, salt and pepper to taste*

Method: 1. Partially bone the goose thighs, open them and season them with a ground-up mixture of garlic, rosemary, raisins, salt, and pepper; close them and truss with twine.

2. Brown the thighs for 3-4 minutes in a dressing of olive oil and butter in a small copper pan; then add the thyme and finish cooking in the oven at 390°F/ 200°C for at least 20 minutes.

3. When the thighs are cooked, remove the fat and pour over the red wine; place the hob and allow the wine to evaporate, then add the balsamic vinegar and the roux, reduce for a few minutes, then remove the thighs and keep them hot.

4. Arrange the thighs on the plates, partially carving them to form a fan-shape and decorating with the tip of the bone. Accompany with potatoes, carrots, zucchini, and broccoli, garnish with the sauce and decorate with pine kernels, flakes of chocolate, and thyme leaves. Serve very hot.

Wines:

*Gutturnio
or Rosso del Salento*

Gianni Bolzoni

FOIE GRAS

Escalopes of foie gras

Serves 4

14 oz/400 g raw goose foie gras, cut into thick slices, 2 tbsp Marsala, a few drops of raspberry wine vinegar, 1 knob of goose fat, salt, white pepper

Method: 1. Melt a little goose fat in a non-stick iron frying pan; add the Marsala and the vinegar, reduce for a few moments, then place the slices of *foie gras* in the pan and sear for a few minutes on both sides; add a little pepper and salt lightly.
2. Serve on a bed of potato purée lightly flavoured with white truffle.

Wines:
Traminer di Lavis,
Terre di Franciacorta, or
Cabernet Sauvignon/Merlot

FOIE GRAS

Foie gras with Savoy cabbage

Serves four

4 slices of fresh foie gras, weighing about 2½ oz/70 g each, 7 oz/200 g Savoy cabbage, 3½ tbsp/50 g butter, 2 tbsp roux, ½ glass Port,
1 black truffle, weighing about 1¾ oz/50 g, salt, pepper, sugar

Method: 1. Finely chop the Savoy cabbage and sauté in a frying pan over a medium heat, in part of the butter with a little salt, sugar, and pepper; ensure the cabbage stays slightly crunchy.
2. While the cabbage is cooking, prepare the sauce: finely chop the truffle; pour the Port into a small saucepan, add the chopped truffle, reduce, then add the roux and thicken with a little butter.
3. Salt and pepper the slices of *foie gras* and cook them briefly in a non-stick frying pan without adding any fat.

Cook them quickly on both sides, then pat the escalopes dry with absorbent paper.
4. Serve the *foie gras* on a bed of savoy cabbage, and pour over the truffle sauce.

Wines:
Recioto di Gambellara
or Zola Predosa Terre Rosse Malmsey

FOIE GRAS

Ambrosia of cold roast goose foie gras

Serves six

22 raw goose foie gras, weighing 1½ lb/700 g each
For the mostarda: a generous 1 lb/500 g squash, 3 carrots, 1 fresh pineapple, 3 apples, 2 pears, 2 cloves of garlic, ¼ cup/50 g raisins,
a pinch/⅔ g peppercorns and juniper berries, 1 chilli pepper, 1⅔ cups/400 g cane sugar, ¾ cup/200 ml white wine vinegar

Method: 1. Cut the *foie gras* into slices about ½ in/1 cm thick and grill for 3 minutes on both sides.
2. Arrange the slices of roast *foie gras* in a porcelain terrine, cover with greaseproof paper and press under a 2 lb/1 kg weight. Chill in the refrigerator for 48 hours.
3. Clean and dice all the fruit and vegetables. Boil the vinegar with the sugar, and add all the ingredients one at a time. Cook for 1 hour 30 minutes. Cool.

4. Serve the terrine of *foie gras* cut into slices with brioche and mostarda.

NB: There is a recipe for brioche on page 53.

Wines:

Liqueur-style red Recioto
or Natural Chambave muscatel

FOIE GRAS

Escalopes of foie gras with balsamic vinegar

Serves four

14 oz/400 g foie gras, cut into 4 escalopes, 4 red turnips, a dash of balsamic vinegar, salt, white pepper

Method: 1. Cut the red turnips into thin shreds and parboil.
2. Quickly sauté the escalopes of *foie gras* in a non-stick frying pan; towards the end of cooking, season with freshly ground white pepper, a dash of balsamic vinegar, and salt.
3. Serve the *foie gras* on a bed of red turnip and sprinkle over the cooking juices.

Wines:

*Malvoisie de Nus
or Zola Predosa Italian Terre Rosse Riesling*

DESSERTS

Decorative Easter focaccia loaf

Makes 1 focaccia loaf

2 tsp/10 g brewers' yeast, a generous 3 cups/500 g flour, 3 goose eggs, 6½ tbsp/100 g superfine sugar, ⅓ cup/80 g butter, 1 tsp/5 g salt,
1 tsp/5 g peanut oil, the zest of 1 lemon, milk as required

Method: 1. Dissolve the yeast in some milk.
2. Soften the butter and zest the lemon. Mix 2 eggs with the sugar, add the flour, the softened butter, the salt, the oil, the yeast dissolved in milk, and the grated lemon zest; mix thoroughly and knead the mixture until it forms a smooth, even dough. Leave to rise.
3. When the dough has risen , divide into two parts, one much bigger than the other, and then divide both of these parts into three equal parts each. The three smaller parts should be used to make a scarf, cowl and Franciscan-style cord for the "friar", while the three larger parts are to be made into a plait. Place a raw goose egg at the beginning of the plait and secure it with the cowl and scarf prepared earlier; be sure to leave part of the egg uncovered. Form the cord from the third small piece of dough and tie it about half-way along the plait.

4. Leave the whole loaf to rise again and brush lightly with melted butter.
5. Bake at 355°F/180°C for about 35 minutes. Remove from the oven. Allow to cool, then paint the egg to look like a friar's face.

Wine

Ramandolo

Sweet goose liver mousse in raspberry and grappa sauce

Serves ten

14 oz/400 g goose liver, thoroughly cleaned, with all fat and bile removed, ½ cup plus 2 tbsp/150 g sugar, 1¼ cup/300 g fior di latte cheese, the zest of 1 lemon, 7 sheets of isinglass (fish glue), 2 cups/300 g raspberries, 6 ½ tbsp/100 ml grappa, 2 tbsp sugar
For the garnish: pine kernels, raisins, fresh mint leaves

Method: 1. Cut the liver into pieces and rinse under running water for 30 minutes, then parboil and set aside.

2. Soften the isinglass in water and squeeze it out. Heat the *fior di latte* cheese but do not allow it to bubble; add the sugar, the softened and squeezed out isinglass, and the goose liver, and blend all the ingredients together in the mixer for a few seconds, adding the lemon zest. Pour into little pudding molds and place in the refrigerator for 2 hours.

3. While the mousse is chilling, heat the raspberries into a saucepan with the grappa and the sugar; strain the moment it comes to the boil. Soak the raisins.

4. Cover the bottom of each plate with the raspberry sauce and arrange the sweet pudding on top, garnished with pine kernels, raisins and fresh mint leaves. Serve.

Wines:

*White Mezzocorona muscatel
or Recioto di Soave*

Chefs and restaurants who have contributed to this book

Roberto Andreoni
Ristorante VIA DEL BORGO
viale della Libertà, 136
20049 Concorezzo (MI)

Bruno Barbieri
Locanda SOLAROLA
via Santa Croce, 5
40023 Castel Guelfo (BO)

Sergio Bartolucci
Ristorante EUROSSOLA
piazza Stazione, 36
28037 Domodossola (VB)

Piero Bertinotti
Ristorante PINOCCHIO
via Matteotti, 147
28021 Borgomanero (NO)

Walter Bianconi
Ristorante TIVOLI
via Lacedel, 34
32043 Cortina d'Ampezzo (BL)

Luca Bolfo e Mario Oriani
Ristorante
VECCHIO MULINO
via al Monumento 5
27012 Certosa di Pavia (PV)

Gianni Bolzoni
Trattoria DEL FULMINE
via Carioni, 12
26017 Trescore Cremasco (CR)

Luigi Bortolini
Ristorante "DA GIGETTO"
via A. De Gasperi, 4
31050 Miane (TV)

Giorgio Busdon
Albergo Ristorante
ASTORIA ITALIA
Piazza XX Settembre, 24
33100 Udine

Giovanni Cannavò
Hotel ristorante CAPARENA
via Nazionale, 189
98039 Taormina (ME)

Roberto Canton
Ristorante Albergo
LA PRIMULA
via San Rocco, 47
33080 San Quirino (PN)

Sergio Carboni
Albergo Ristorante ITALIA
via Garibaldi, 1
26038 Torre de Picenardi (CR)

Silvana Chiabai
GIUDITTA TERESA
FORNO DI PASTICCERIA
33049 San Pietro al Natisone (UD)

Filippo Chiappini Dattilo
ANTICA OSTERIA
DEL TEATRO
via Verdi, 16
29100 Piacenza (PC)

Georges Cogny
Locanda CANTONIERA
via Provinciale, 1
29023 Farini d'Olmo (PC)

Igles Corelli
Locanda della TAMERICE
via Argine Mezzano, 2
44020 Ostellato (FE)

Gianni Cosetti
Hotel ristorante ROMA
piazza XX Settembre, 14
33028 Tolmezzo (UD)

Roberto Cozzarolo
Trattoria "DA TONI"
via Sentinis, 1
33030 Gradiscutta di Varmo (UD)

Enzo De Prà
Ristorante Albergo DOLADA
via Dolada, 21
32010 Plois in Pieve
d'Alpago (BL)

Enrico Derflinger
Hotel EDEN
via Ludovisi, 49
00187 Roma

Margherita Falzoni
Ristorante PARIS
via Cavour, 69
27024 Cilavegna (PV)

Edoardo Fantasma
Trattoria GUALLINA
Fraz. Guallina
via Molino Faenza, 19
27036 Mortara (PV)

Corrado Fasolato
Ristorante LA SIRIOLA
loc. Armentarola
in Pre de Vi, 127
39030 San Cassiano (BZ)

Herbert Hintner
Ristorante ZUR ROSE
via J. Innerhofer, 2
39057 Appiano (BZ)

Ernst Knam
L'ANTICA ARTE DEL DOLCE
via A. Anfossi, 10
20135 Milano

Franco Luise
via Bosco Wollenborg, 17/A
35124 Padova (PD)

Luigi Mariani
Ristorante "CASCINA BOVILE"
27030 Ceretto Lomellina (PV)

Sergio Mei
HOTEL FOUR SEASONS
via Gesù, 8
20121 Milano

Valentino Marcattilii
Ristorante SAN DOMENICO
via Gaspare Sacchi, 1
40026 Imola (BO)

Davide Oldani
Ristorante GIANNINO
via A. Sciesa, 8
20135 Milano

Lucio Pompili
Ristorante SYMPOSIUM
QUATTRO STAGIONI
via Cartoceto, 38
61030 Cartoceto (PS)

Germano Pontoni
via Aquileia, 17
33037 Pasian di Prato (UD)

Claudio Prandi
Ristorante
IL GRISO
22040 Malgrate (LC)

Romano Resen
Hotel PRINCIPE DI SAVOIA
piazza della Repubblica, 32
20124 Milano

Claudio Sadler
Ristorante SADLER
via Troilo, 14
20143 Milano (MI)

Ezio Santin
ANTICA OSTERIA
DEL PONTE
piazza G. Negri, 9
20080 Cassinetta
di Lugagnano (MI)

Nadia Santini
Ristorante DAL PESCATORE
46013 Runate di Canneto
sull'Oglio (MN)

Romano Tamani
Ristorante AMBASCIATA
via Martiri di Belfiore, 33
46026 Quistello (MN)

Fabio Testa
"Evoluzione Gastronomica"
via Milano, 5
40139 Bologna

Umberto Vezzoli
Hotel PALACE,
CASANOVA GRILL
piazza della Repubblica, 20
20124 Milano

Luigi Zago
Locanda alle OFFICINE
via Nazionale, 46/48
33042 Buttrio (UD)

We would also like to thank all those who contributed to the writing of this book. Special thanks to:
Marina Danieli,
Franco Mesturini,
Gioacchino Palestro,
Bertilla Pontoni,
Annamaria Russo Toffolini,
Dott.ssa Paola Salvatori,
Dott.ssa Francesca Tamburlini
della Biblioteca Comunale
V. Joppi di Udine
and la Ditta Jolanda de Colò
di Aiello del Friuli.

STARTERS

FIRST COURSES AND SINGLE DISHES

MAIN COURSES

FOIE GRAS

DESSERTS
(AND SAVORY TARTS)